RIBBON
EMBROIDERY

RIBBON
EMBROIDERY

DAPHNE J. ASHBY & JACKIE WOOLSEY

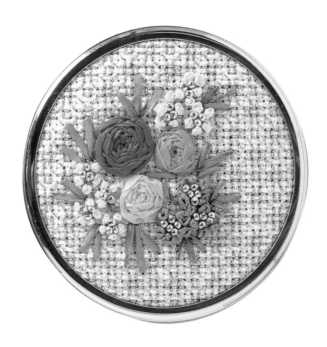

David & Charles

DEDICATION

I should like to dedicate this book to Ann Sumner and the late Trudie

Anderton, who first introduced me to ribbon embroidery and to my

husband, Hedley, without whose help, patience and support this book

would not have been possible

DAPHNE J. ASHBY

A DAVID & CHARLES BOOK

First published in the UK in 1996

Copyright © Daphne J. Ashby & Jackie Woolsey 1996
Photography by Di Lewis and Paul Biddle

Daphne J. Ashby and Jackie Woolsey have asserted their right to be
identified as authors of this work in accordance with the Copyright,
Designs and Patents Act, 1988.

A catalogue record for this book is available from the British Library.

ISBN 0 7153 0433 X
Book design by Annie Moss
Mac artwork by John Fowler
Printed in Great Britain by
Butler & Tanner Ltd, Frome
for David & Charles
Brunel House Newton Abbot Devon

Contents

Introduction

Today's upsurge of interest in using ribbon as an embellishment for creative embroidery, either applied to the surface or stitched through the fabric, owes much to the increasing availability of types and colours of ribbon as well as to the development of new ways of handling it.

Embroidered decoration using ribbons was a feature of women's fashion in the early years of the nineteenth century but was replaced by patterned materials in the 1820s. With the move to plain silk fabrics for dresses in the 1840s, when the shape of the dress became more important than its decoration, accessories such as sachets, muffs, gloves, bags and parasols, were decorated with silk embroidery, aerophane, chenille and China ribbons. These ribbons were made from silk only ⅛ in wide, shaded widthways from dark to light; but, by the end of the century they were only available in plain colours.

During the early Victorian period, ribbon flowers were used to decorate clothing as well as cushions, cards and other items. Later, in the 1880s, China ribbons were combined with chenille thread and coloured silks, a technique known as Rococo embroidery. Design transfers and kits became available, as did ribbons from other parts of Europe, America and the Far East.

In the early 1980's, Daphne had the chance to study the way the Victorians had handled ribbons to produce the gathered and stitched flowers which decorated much mid-nineteenth century fashion, and this was to inspire her to explore and discover new ways of using ribbons in embroidery.

Apart from intermittent flurries of interest in the first quarter of this century, it is only since the early 1990s that ribbon embroidery has gained a firm place as part of the embroiderer's increasing repertoire. In this book, we guide you through the range of ribbons which are currently on the market and give you the opportunity to study and learn the basic techniques required to embroider with ribbon. Samplers and careful step-by-step instructions, accompanied by detail photographs give you a clear and thorough grounding in this fascinating craft.

Starting with the simplest single gathered ribbon flowers, the projects increase in complexity to involve woven roses and combining ribbon embroidery with other surface embroidery and stitching techniques. Later in the book, ribbons are also stitched through the fabric in combination with delightful backgrounds of counted-thread stitches.

The sections on fabrics and design sources are all aimed at inviting even beginners to attempt the fascinating art of embellishing embroidery with ribbons. We hope that experimenting with the various techniques and projects illustrated in words and pictures throughout this book will give you pleasure in the embroidery as well as the satisfaction of finished pieces with your own original interpretation.

Materials

Measurements for materials are given in both imperial and metric. Use one system or the other consistently throughout a project – do not mix the measurements as, although equivalent, they are not always exactly equal. Certain products are only available in specific measurements and equivalents cannot be given; e.g. Kreinik ribbon is only sold in widths of ⅛in or ¹⁄₁₆in.

FABRICS FOR BACKGROUNDS

Ribbons can be worked on any type of fabric that is firm and capable of being stretched and laced over card. Silk, cotton, satin and taffeta are all suitable and, of course, with fabrics like satin, either side can be used.

Any fine fabrics that would be unsuitable on their own can be backed with cotton: simply tack (baste) the two fabrics together before starting the embroidery and work through the two layers. As this will be a permanent bond, great care must be taken when stretching the finished work.

EVENWEAVES
If you want to combine ribbon work with counted thread and canvas work stitches, the background fabric needs to be specially woven. Evenweave fabrics have the same number of threads in the warp and the weft, and are particularly suitable. There is a wide range available, such as Congress Cloth (or Coin Net), Jobelin and Charles Craft, Aida and hardanger.

RIBBON
Wide ribbon can be used as a background fabric, sewn on to a cotton backing. Narrower ribbon can be woven into a fabric, then applied to a cotton backing before working the embroidery.

RIBBONS

The variety of types and colours of ribbon available to today's embroiderer is enormous; names and addresses of the manufacturers whose products are used in this book can be found on page 126.

Narrow ribbon is more suitable for gathered ribbon petals, woven roses and for actual embroidery, such as French knots and satin stitch. Wider ribbon tends to be used for couching or binding and can even be joined together to make background fabrics.

Different effects can be achieved with different types of narrow ribbon. Gathered ribbon petals in silk or new embroidery ribbon give a softer look than in double-faced satin ribbon. You can produce a more sculptured effect when you weave satin ribbon if you fold it over between each action of the weaving.

Pure silk ribbons tend to fray more than the synthetic ones, so do ensure that the ends are well tucked-in.

THREAD

A number of different types of thread are used in our projects, and it is important to use the particular one specified since each has its special purpose.

EMBROIDERY THREADS
Various companies produce their own ranges of embroidery threads and these are interchangeable, as they have equivalent ranges of colours. Use relatively short lengths of thread – not more than 15in (38cm) – to avoid the thread 'thinning' as it passes repeatedly through canvas or fabric. The number of threads to use in your needle is specified in the project instructions.
Coton Perlé: a soft, twisted thread which comes in a

good variety of colours and thicknesses.

Coton à Broder: a very smooth, single stranded thread, not widely known, which gives stitches a strong definition. It makes a perfect basis for the woven roses.

Stranded cotton (floss): consists of six threads which can be used together or separated into strands to be used singly or in any combination.

SEWING THREADS

These are used for gathering the ribbons as well as for ordinary sewing. As only minimal amounts are needed they are not always listed separately. Match the colour of your sewing thread as closely as possible to the ribbon so that the stitches are hidden.

RAYON THREADS

These shiny and brightly coloured threads, mainly imported from India, give a delightful sparkle to a piece of work. They are very fine and often used in combinations of up to six threads in the needle.

A wide variety of ribbons are available to today's embroiderer

METALLIC THREADS

These synthetic metal threads are used for stitching, like an embroidery or sewing thread. As metallic threads can 'fray' at the ends, work with a double thread in your needle. Using two thicknesses of a finer thread gives the same effect as a single thicker thread. After threading the needle, allow the two ends to hang level. Hold the threads at the needle end, run your fingers down the length of the threads and then release. This allows any twist to unravel. Then, knot the ends together, avoiding another twist by laying the threads in a loop over your finger and stitching through it twice.

Never use a doubled metallic thread longer than approximately 15in (38cm).

BEADS AND BEADING

Adding beads undoubtedly enhances a finished piece, bringing sparkle to the work. The tiny beads (by Beadesign) used in the majority of our projects are intended for 14-count fabric but an even smaller bead, intended for 18-count fabric, has now been added to the range.

You need to use a very fine needle to attach such small beads, and special, long beading needles are available. However, you may find it easier to use a fine quilting needle, which is far shorter, instead. See Stitching, page 115 for instructions.

VILENE

This company produces a range of interfacing from which we use two particular types. Both can be cut to exact shapes without fraying.

Vilene extra heavy interfacing: A particularly stiff type of Vilene, extremely useful as a backing for embroidered fabrics, particularly when mounting in cards, pictures or on a box

Iron-on Vilene: Much finer than the above, this is available in various weights and is bonded to the back of a fabric, using an iron. Fabrics backed with iron-on Vilene can be cut without fraying; backed knitted fabrics are much easier to work.

CARDBOARD

Greyboard: a heavy duty card available in a variety of thicknesses and large sheets from arts and craft suppliers. It is used for box-making, and as the basic card over which to lace fabrics.

Mounting board: a thinner, faced board, which can also be used for lacing fabrics before framing. It comes in many different colours and finishes, and is primarily used as the card from which an aperture is cut to surround and enhance pictures.

Thin card: usually only used for linings. You can buy it in art and craft shops (ask for card weighing around 250gsm), or use cereal packaging instead.

EQUIPMENT

NEEDLES

Tapestry: Has a blunt end and is normally used for canvaswork and counted thread embroidery. Its main use in this book is for weaving ribbon and using ribbon like a thread on canvas.

Embroidery: A sharp needle with a fairly large eye which can take a variety of threads. Used in this book for many purposes but particularly with a sewing thread for gathered ribbons.

Beading: A long, very fine needle, specifically for attaching beads.

Sharp: A fine, sharp multipurpose sewing needle.

Curved needles: Excellent for ladder stitching fabric-covered card surfaces together; particularly useful in box making.

SCISSORS

You will need a large pair of sharp scissors for cutting fabrics, and a small, very sharp, pair of scissors for cutting embroidery threads. Do try to keep your scissors for their specific purposes.

Working with Ribbon

Ribbon embroidery is relatively easy to master and, as with all creative arts,
time taken to practice the various techniques will reap its own reward.
If you're new to ribbon embroidery do read through this section and try
out the techniques before you start a project.
The effects of working with ribbon are varied and stunning. Yet all this is achieved
with only two main techniques: working the ribbon on the surface of the fabric; and
stitching the ribbon through the fabric, as if it were thread.

SURFACE RIBBON EMBROIDERY

In this book we have mainly used two methods of surface ribbon embroidery: gathering ribbon to make individual flowers or petals; and weaving ribbon around wheel-like stitches to create rounded, raised roses.

GATHERED RIBBON FLOWERS

Single gathered ribbon petals: To make single gathered ribbon petals, use any kind of 3 or 4mm ribbon cut into 1¼in (3cm) lengths. Thread a needle with cotton to match the colour of the ribbon, and pull it through until it is double. Bring the needle up through the fabric you're embroidering at the position of the first petal of the flower, and refer to the photograph, right.

First, gather the ribbon on to the needle (1). Push the needle down in the middle of the ribbon ⅛in (3mm) from one end. Take the needle along ¼in (6mm) and make a small stitch along one edge of the ribbon. Repeat this at the other side and continue, bringing the needle up ⅛in (3mm) from the end of the ribbon.

Hold the ribbon and needle vertically between your thumb and forefinger and turn it so that the ribbon ends are facing upwards. Pull the needle through, taking the ribbon down to the fabric. Put the needle through its first entry point in the ribbon and back through the fabric (2), ensuring that the ribbon ends sit on top of each other. As you pull, the ribbon will gather to make the petal (3); secure on the reverse with a back stitch.

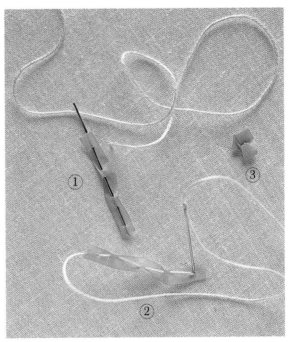

Working a single gathered ribbon petal

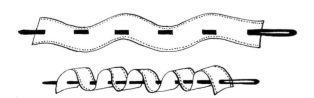

FIGURE 1 *Gathering the ribbon on the needle*

The sampler, right, shows how you can combine single gathered petals to create a variety of effects as described below:

Round flowers: These are made up from five gathered ribbon petals, filling the centres with French knots or beads, or both.

Oval flowers: Made up from seven or nine gathered ribbon petals arranged in oval shapes. Three straight stitches, forming arrow head shapes, around the outside of the oval suggest additional outer flat petals. The centre is filled with French knots or beads, or both. The French knots could be made from thread or either silk or 100% polyester ribbon – see Oval Mauves, page 48.

Double (round or oval) flowers: Made up from two concentric circles or ovals of gathered ribbon petals with centres of French knots or beads, or both. You may like to use different coloured ribbons for the circles, a deeper shade for the inner row, to give a contrast.

Tall flowers: Made up from a series of single gathered ribbon petals on alternate sides of an imaginary stem, with added French knots and small straight green stitches to suggest foliage.

Single gathered 7mm ribbon petals: Ideal if made up in silk or 100% polyester ribbon, gathered as described on page 11, and secured with a French knot made in thread. For examples of these in use, see Framed by Flowers, page 77.

WOVEN RIBBON ROSES

These are easier to work if the background fabric is not too closely woven. Refer to the photograph on page 13 for a step-by-step guide to weaving the flowers.

Using a single Coton à Broder type of thread – not stranded cotton (floss) – sew a series of seven straight stitches, each about ¼in (6mm) long, meeting at a central point to form the spokes of a wheel (1). This is the foundation wheel around which you weave ribbon to create a rose.

Bring the weaving ribbon (approximately 3mm or 4mm wide) up through the fabric (2) and begin to weave under and over the spokes around the wheel (3). Pull the

SINGLE GATHERED
RIBBON PETAL

ROUND FLOWER

DOUBLE OVAL FLOWER

ROUND FLOWER

TALL FLOWER

Single gathered ribbon petals can be combined to create a variety of different shaped flowers as shown above, with the addition of stitched details.

ribbon firmly at first and then more loosely towards the outside (4). Work as many rows as are needed to cover the spokes, then take the ribbon through to the back of the work and back stitch through the spokes on the reverse to finish off (5).

To keep the ribbon free from twists, hold it over the forefinger of the hand not holding the needle. This will also give you control over positioning the ribbon.

When you become practised with this weaving method, you may find that you can achieve better shapes by twisting the ribbon before going over and

Working a woven ribbon rose

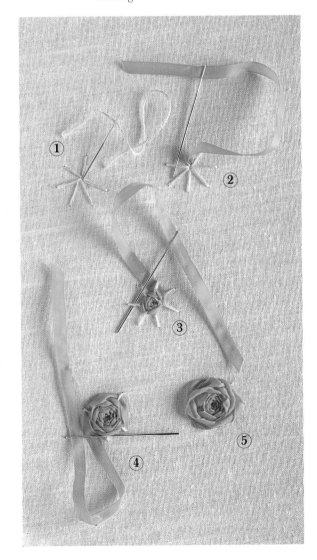

under the next two spokes. Experiment to see the different effects that can be obtained by keeping the ribbon smooth or allowing it to twist once.

STITCHING WITH RIBBON

Taking the ribbon through the fabric to make actual stitches lets you create some wonderful effects. Like the other techniques, stitching requires practice to perfect and you need to handle the ribbon carefully to avoid twists. That is why it's important to consider your choice of materials. For example, the holes in canvas make ribbon stitching easy. To work with finer woven materials, however, it's best to stitch with 'soft' ribbons – silk or 100% polyester. In all our projects the materials we recommend are tried and tested.

To avoid using a bulky knot when starting to stitch with ribbon, bring the needle up through the fabric or canvas, make a small stitch and then return to the back, passing the needle through the centre of the ribbon. To finish off, thread ribbon securely through stitching on the back of the work.

Practice guiding the ribbon with the forefinger of your free hand to prevent it twisting. It's easier to avoid twists than try to straighten them out later.

The sampler on page 14 shows some of the effects that can be achieved described below. Many flowers not covered in this book can be formed using straight stitches, and a study of flower petals and shapes will undoubtedly inspire you to embroider your own variations.

Half daisies: Formed by stitching fans of irregular length straight stitches, all appearing to come from a central point.

Full daisies: To allow for perspective, the straight stitches at the rear should be shorter than those in the foreground.

Foliage: Fans of straight stitches can be arranged to suggest foliage. For leaves, work straight stitches, overlapping each other, on alternate sides of an imaginary line and vary the length of stitch.

When handling ribbons it is very important to ensure that they are laid correctly. If the stitch being used doesn't specifically ask for the ribbon to be twisted, always lay the full face of the ribbon to the fabric.

Only thread comparatively short lengths of ribbon through the needle to avoid twisting.

USING A FRAME

If you are going to use an embroidery frame, always make sure that the frame is large enough to contain the whole design. You need plenty of room so that the stitching doesn't come too close to the edges and become distorted. The ideal frame size is suggested for each project but it is always possible to use a larger frame by adding a cotton border to the fabric to be embroidered.

Always centre the work in the frame and ensure that the design is placed on the straight grain of the fabric – otherwise, you could come across difficulties when you stretch the finished piece.

If you use a small 'precious' piece of fabric which is adequate for the embroidery but not large enough to fit into a frame, stitch it on to a larger piece of cotton fabric and, from the back, cut away the cotton fabric inside the stitched line. You can also use this procedure to make working on canvas in a circular frame easier.

RECTANGULAR EMBROIDERY FRAMES

Attach the fabric to the frame as tightly as possible using staples or drawing pins. If you use drawing pins, cover the heads with masking tape to stop the embroidery threads catching on them.

NOTE: Scroll or roller frames are not suitable for ribbon embroidery.

This sampler shows how effectively ribbon can create flowers and foliage by stitching the ribbon through the fabric

A partly-worked embroidery. Work with the frame upside down for a ready-made container for small ribbon pieces.

CIRCULAR EMBROIDERY FRAMES

Bind the inner ring of the circular frame with cotton tape before stretching the fabric very tightly between the rings. This helps to hold the fabric firmly.

If you work with the frame upside down you have a ready-made container to hold small pieces of ribbon and beads.

TRANSFERRING THE DESIGN ON TO THE FABRIC

In most cases the designs for each project are provided as templates. Some projects also have stitch charts for counted embroidery and canvaswork. The designs for ribbon embroidery, however, cannot be counted out on to the fabric, and so have to be transferred. It may help to photocopy the design from the book and transfer the design from the photocopy, using one of the following methods:

1. Place the design underneath the fabric and, holding the work up to a light source (eg taped to a window pane), carefully mark the relevant lines with a sharp pencil;

2. Make holes along the design lines on the photocopy, place the sheet on top of the fabric and mark through the holes with a pencil;

3. Trace the design on to tracing paper and put this on top of the fabric. Stitch along the design lines through the fabric. Remove the tracing paper, leaving the stitched lines.

WARNING: Never use a ball point pen. Fabric marker pens are only intended to be used on man-made fabrics; the long-term effects of marker pen chemicals are unknown.

DESIGNS AND DESIGN SOURCES

Essentially, designs for ribbon embroidery are based on the shapes of flowers: round, oval, double-oval and tall flowers. As in the art of flower arranging, the heavier round flowers take a central position in the design, with the daintier and taller flowers all round. Similarly, the darker colours should be in the middle of the design and the lighter shades towards the outside.

The different types of ribbon and the different ways of using them give great variations in texture, and this can be enhanced by hand-stitching, machine stitching and canvaswork stitches.

Sources of ideas for embroidery using ribbons are all around. Books on flower arranging often contain useful small pencil drawings, and the flower arrangements themselves are based on classic design shapes - symmetrical and asymmetrical triangles, circles, crescents, curves, the Hogarth curve and L-shape, all of which translate well into embroidery. Greetings cards for all occasions feature flower designs, particularly Mother's Day, Easter, birthdays and Christmas cards. During the festive season, even the decorations themselves can inspire.

Wrapping paper, floral fabrics, wallpaper and decorated china very often include flowers in their designs and areas can be adapted and incorporated into ribbon embroidery projects.

The list is endless and Nature is a design inspiration in herself. It may be that just looking out of your window or walking around a garden will fire your imagination and you will have all you need to start designing your own individual piece of ribbon embroidery.

Wherever your inspiration comes from, work at your design sketches until you are happy with the composition, then choose your colours carefully to tone or contrast, depending on the effect you want to achieve. Don't overwork your design trying to achieve perfection; you can still develop it as you stitch the actual embroidery.

Every now and then, hold your work at arm's length to take in the effect of the whole design. Then you will see whether an extra stitch or flower would enhance the overall effect.

Sewing Set

GATHERED RIBBON FLOWERS
WITH RIBBON WORK AND BEADING

Future collectors of needlework ephemera will delight to add these items to their collections. The laid and couched flat ribbons, in a glorious range of colours, are aligned to give a rainbow effect, with beads adding a sparkle. Gathered ribbon flowers nestle in the central squares, surrounded by massed French knots, and the hand-made braid and tassels add a special touch.

Materials
(to make the complete set)

- Beiersbont Netherlands Check in pale green, 19¾ x 15¾in (50 x 40cm). This fabric is very wide and the amount needed is half of a 'fat quarter'
- Cotton lining fabric, patterned or plain, for backing the needlecase and scissors holder

OFFRAY EMBROIDERY RIBBON,
ONE CARD EACH OF:

2mm	Pastel green 513	4mm	Ultra violet 467
	Ultra violet 467		Grape 463
	Grape 463		Daffodil 645
	Daffodil 645		Ivory 810
	Ivory 810		
	Light orchid 430		

ANCHOR COTON À BRODER,
ONE SKEIN EACH OF:

Yellow 305	Pink 970
Mauve 108	White 001

- Panda polyester lamé silver 2, 3mm wide, 4½ yd (4m)
- Vilene extra heavy interfacing: 10in (25.5cm) square for the needlecase; 6¼ x 4¾ in (16 x 12cm) rectangle for the scissors holder
- Felt in white, 8¼in (21 cm) square
- Kreinik silver cord 001C, one reel
- Gütermann sewing thread to match fabric, one reel
- Beadesign beads, one packet of Topaz 197
- Mounting card
- Double-sided tape and wide parcel tape
- Foam pad for the pin cushion, 3¾ x 3¾ x 1½in (9.5 x 9.5 x 4 cm)

Equipment

- Embroidery frame, 10in (25.5 cm) circular
- No. 24 tapestry needle for weaving
- No. 7 embroidery needle
- Beading needle
- Embroidery scissors

Needlecase

On its own, or as part of the set, this beautifully worked needlecase is both functional and decorative.

PREPARATION

Cut two pieces of the Beiersbont Netherlands fabric, one 4¾in (12cm) square and the other 10¼ x 7in (26 x 18cm). Be careful to centre the pattern on the check of the fabric. If you are making the matching set, fig. 1 on page 19 shows how to place the shapes for the three projects on one piece of fabric. Put the smaller piece of fabric into the circular frame and stretch tightly.

STITCHING

RIBBON EMBROIDERY
See Working with Ribbon, page 11. Refer often to the photograph of the finished piece (pages 18 and 20) for

positioning the ribbon. The four central squares are for the ribbon flowers. The squares that surround the flower squares are for weaving the ribbon.

Weaving: Start with the ultra violet 2mm ribbon and thread this into the tapestry needle. Come up through the fabric to begin weaving down the left side of the large outside square. The weaving is done under the white stitching which is part of the fabric. Make sure that the ribbon always lies flat. Go back down through the fabric at the bottom and come up on the side of that square ready to weave along the bottom. Then do the right-hand side and finally the top.

Repeat this procedure with each 2mm coloured ribbon in turn: grape, light orchid, daffodil and ivory. In the corner squares, weave the ribbons through each other as they cross over.

Silver ribbon: Leaving about 1in (2.5cm) of spare ribbon at each end, lay the silver ribbon over the line of the white fabric stitches by the side of the first woven ribbon. Couch the silver ribbon with Kreinik silver thread over each intersection of the white stitching on the fabric and add one small bead. Refer to the photograph of the finished item, add the other silver ribbons and attach with beads (see Stitching, page 115 for beading instructions).

Gathered ribbon flowers: Work the flowers with five pieces of 4mm ribbon each. Refer to the photograph on page 20 for the placing of the colours.

Ribbon French knots: Add 2mm daffodil yellow ribbon French knots for the centres of the flowers, then finally surround each flower with 2mm green ribbon French knots to fill the square. Ribbon French knots are worked in exactly the same way as the thread ones (see Stitching, page 118).

FINISHING AND MAKING UP

Cut a 3¼in (8.5cm) square of mounting card and lay it centrally over the back of the stitching and, using a double thread, lace across the back. (See Presentation, page 120, for lacing instructions.)

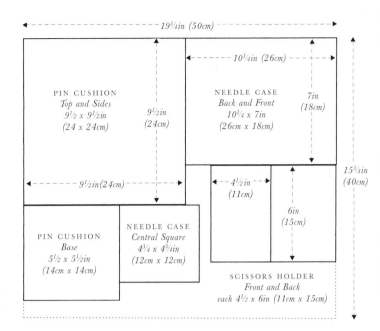

FIGURE 1   *Cutting plan for fabric.*

Cut a piece of Vilene 9 x 4¾in (23 x 12cm) and lay it over the reverse side of the larger piece of fabric. Fold the edges of the fabric over the Vilene and secure by using herring bone stitch along each edge, mitring each corner as you come to it. Turn the work over and fold in half. Position the stitched square centrally on one half, marking this carefully. Place the fabric flat and stitch the finished square in position on the right side of the fabric, stitching through both the fabric and the Vilene.

Line the whole of the wrong side of the work with cotton material. Cut the 8¼in (21cm) square of white felt in half, using pinking shears, and pink the edges also. Then attach these two felt pages to the middle of the case, through the lining, to take the needles.

The cord: There are two ways of making the cord from Coton à Broder thread.

METHOD 1: Take two lengths of each colour – eight lengths in all – and knot at each end. Twist until taut and then double over and allow the two halves to twist together.

METHOD 2: (making a firmer cord by using an old hand drill): Knot the ends of the threads as above and place one end over a support – the reel-holder on a

Detail of the neeedlecase ribbon embroidery

KNOTTED CORD   LOOPS   WRAPPING

F I G U R E   2   *Making a tassel*

sewing machine is fine; alternatively, use a lever door handle. In place of the usual drill bit, put a cup hook into the drill. Loop the other end of the skein of threads over the cup hook and turn the handle until the threads are tightly twisted. Take the loop from the cup hook and place it over the support with the other ends of the threads and, running your finger along to find halfway, hook this point over the cup hook and turn the drill handle backwards. This will give a locked twist to the cord. Remove the cord from the support and allow it to untwist.

The cord goes around the spine of the needle case and the ends are positioned at the bottom edge and knotted.

The tassel: See fig. 2. Take one thread of each of the four colours and thread them into the blunt needle. Holding the ends of the knotted cord in your left hand, plus the ends of the threads that you have just threaded, keep passing the needle over the knot, making a series of loops about 1½in (4cm) long until most of the thread has been used. The knot should now be hidden by the threads. Cut off the remaining threads and use these to wrap around the threads directly below the knot, finishing off securely and creating a tassel. Trim the lower ends of the tassel neatly.

Pin Cushion

What could be more useful to the busy stitcher? Eminently practical, our pin cushion also makes an attractive addition to any sewing basket. See page 17 for materials and equipment needed.

PREPARATION

Cut two pieces of the Beiersbont Netherlands fabric, one 9½in (24cm) square and the other 5½in (14cm) square. If you're making the matching set follow the cutting plan in fig. 1, page 19.

Cut two squares of mounting card 3¾in (9.5cm) square, and four pieces 1 x 3¾in (2.5 x 9.5cm).

Use the smaller piece of fabric to cover one of the 3¾in (9.5cm) squares of mounting card, and use the double-sided tape to hold this in place. Take the remaining pieces of mounting card (the 3¾in (9.5cm) square and the four pieces, 3¾in (2.5 x 9.5cm), and use them to form a box shape to hold the piece of foam in position. Using parcel tape, fix the four sides to the base and place the foam inside; the foam, being deeper than the container, will stand proud above the box sides, and the covering fabric will press the edges down to give a curved surface.

Stretch the larger piece of fabric tightly into the circular frame.

STITCHING

RIBBON EMBROIDERY

See Working with Ribbon, page 11. Refer often to the photograph of the finished piece on page 18 for positioning the ribbon.

Gathered ribbon flowers: Work the flowers with five pieces of 4mm ribbon each. Refer to the photograph on page 18 for placing the colours.

Ribbon French knots: Add 2mm daffodil yellow ribbon French knots for the centres of the flowers, then finally surround each flower with 2mm green ribbon French knots to fill the square. Ribbon French knots are worked in exactly the same way as the thread ones (see Stitching, page 118).

RIBBON WORK AND BEADING

See Stitching, page 119, for instructions on how to couch ribbon and page 115, for information on beading.

The four flower squares are bordered by silver ribbon. Start at the top left hand corner, tucking the end under as you start to couch the ribbon. Continue to couch the ribbon down to the bottom left-hand corner. To turn the corner, refer to fig. 3. Finish with a straight stitch (1) at the lower edge of the embroidered square; then stitch a diagonal stitch (2) into the corner and fold the ribbon along the line of the stitch, away from the direction in which it will finally lie and make a straight stitch level with the edge of the ribbon (3). Then fold the ribbon the way it is required to lie and stitch another straight stitch (4) to secure before proceeding with the couching along the base of the square. Work each corner in this way and finally, when the ribbon is attached to the top of the square, cut the ribbon and fold under the end and secure. Add small beads at each corner and mid-point of the couched ribbon.

FINISHING AND MAKING UP

Place the fabric upside down over the prepared pin cushion base. Pin the corners, following the line of the box. Remove the fabric from the box and tack and stitch along the line of the corner markings. Trim the turnings and turn the work to the right side.

Place again over the pin cushion base and, before lacing the fabric underneath the box to hold it in position, thread the sides with ribbon, as on the needlecase. Each side should have a complete square for this, with a part square down to the bottom of the box. Start with the ultra violet at the bottom and end with the ivory. Pull the fabric evenly over the base of the pin cushion and lace (see Presentation, page 120), ensuring that you keep the fabric lines straight.

Finally, add the covered base to neaten the finished pin cushion, attaching it carefully with ladder stitching along all four sides. Pull the thread firmly and then your stitches will not show. Avoid the ribbon area when using as a pin cushion.

Scissors Holder

This sumptuously decorated embroidery scissor holder is as delightful as it is useful. See page 17 for materials and equipment needed.

PREPARATION

Cut two pieces of the Beiersbont Netherlands fabric, each 4½ x 6in (11 x 15cm). If you're making the matching set, fig. 1, page 19, shows how to place the shapes on the fabric.

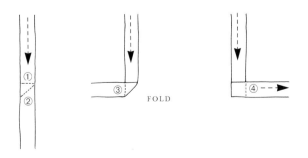

F I G U R E   3   *Turning a corner when couching ribbon*

To enable you to embroider the front section in the embroidery frame, tack (baste) strips of cotton fabric along each edge of one of the pieces of fabric; this will make it large enough to be held in the frame. Stretch this tightly into the circular frame.

STITCHING

RIBBON EMBROIDERY

See Working with Ribbon, page 11. Refer often to the photograph of the finished piece on page 18 for positioning the ribbon. The three central squares are for the ribbon flowers. The squares that surround the flower squares are for weaving the ribbon.

Weaving: Start with the ultra violet 2mm ribbon and thread this into the tapestry needle. Come up through the fabric to begin weaving down the left side of the large outside square. The weaving is done under the white stitching which is part of the fabric. Make sure that the ribbon always lies flat. Go back down through the fabric at the bottom and come up on the side of that square ready, and weave along the bottom. Then do the right-hand side and finally the top.

Repeat this procedure with each 2mm coloured ribbon in turn: grape, light orchid, daffodil and ivory. In the corner squares, weave the ribbons through each other as they cross over. (See the detail photograph of the needlecase on page 20 for arranging the ribbons.)

Silver ribbon: Leaving about 1in (2.5cm) of spare ribbon at each end, lay the silver ribbon over the line of the white fabric stitches by the side of the first woven ribbon. Couch the silver ribbon with Kreinik silver thread over each intersection of the white stitching on the fabric and add one small bead. Referring to the photograph of the finished item on page 18, add the other silver ribbons and attach with beads (see Stitching, page 115, for beading instructions).

Gathered ribbon flowers: Work the flowers with five pieces of 4mm ribbon each. Use ultra violet for the top square, daffodil yellow for the second and grape coloured ribbon for the lower square.

Ribbon French knots: Add 2mm daffodil yellow ribbon French knots for the centres of the flowers, then finally surround each flower with 2mm green ribbon French knots to fill the square. Ribbon French knots are worked in exactly the same way as the thread ones (see Stitching, page 118).

FINISHING AND MAKING UP

As scissors vary in size, you may need to alter the measurements slightly. The scissors in our finished holder measured 4 x 2in (10 x 5cm). For the finished case for this size, a half square was allowed each side of the silver ribbon.

Remove the cotton fabric used to extend the Beiersbont fabric to fit the embroidery frame. Join the embroidered fabric, along one long side only, to the plain fabric, matching the stitching on the fabrics and letting in the silver ribbon. Tack (baste) and machine or hand sew the seam and finger press.

Cut a piece of Vilene 6¼ x 4¾in (16 x 12cm) and place it over the back of the joined fabric pieces. Adjust the size if your scissors vary from that used in the example. Turn in all four raw edges over the Vilene and press.

Cut a piece of lining material ³/₈in (1cm) larger than the Vilene all round, turn under the raw edges, press and lay this over the Vilene. Hem this in place along the top and lower edges. Fold the work in half and oversew the side edges of the lining together.

The cord: Make a cord, as for the needlecase, and place one end centrally, with the knot just below the bottom edge of the scissors holder. The looped end is then taken up through the holder and attached to the scissors. The knot at the lower edge will form the foundation for the tassel.

Ladder stitch down the open side of the holder, just stitching through the outside fabric, and then along the bottom edge, ensuring that the cord is firmly stitched so that the knot cannot slip through. Make the tassel following the instructions on page 20.

Flower Circle

GATHERED RIBBON FLOWERS AND EMBROIDERY

This beautifully delicate and intricate design is a good example of how you can take one idea or motif as a starting point and add to it, letting your inspiration enhance and develop the concept. The central motif was worked from a Victorian ribbon kit produced by Madeira Threads UK Ltd, designed by Daphne. To transform it into the Flower Circle, she then used additional ribbon and threads to work the surrounding garland of flowers, matching and toning colours.

Materials

- Medium weight cotton fabric in cream,
  10in (25.5cm) square

OFFRAY DOUBLE-FACE SATIN RIBBON,
3MM WIDE:
White 029, 20in (50cm)
Cream 815, 39in (1m)
Light orchid 430, 39in (1m)
Purple 465, 39in (1m)
Iris 447, 39in (1m)
Thistle 435, 39in (1m)
Yellow Gold 660, 20in (50cm)

MADEIRA EMBROIDERY SILK,
ONE SKEIN EACH OF:

White	Pale yellow 0112
Cream 1910	Deep yellow 0113
Pale green 1408	Deep mauve 0903
Deep green 1407	

- Coton Perlé, white, one skein
- Vilene extra heavy interfacing, 8in (20cm) square
- Circular mount

Equipment

- Embroidery frame, 8in (20cm) circular
- Embroidery scissors
- No. 7 embroidery needle
- Tracing paper
- Sharp pencil

PREPARATION

Stretch the fabric tightly into the frame. Trace the template and transfer the design to the fabric following the instructions on page 16.

STITCHING

Unless stated, use all four strands of the silk.

RIBBON EMBROIDERY

See Working with Ribbon, page 11. Follow the template carefully and refer often to the photograph of the finished piece on page 23 for positioning the different coloured gathered ribbon flowers.

Gathered ribbon flowers in the centre: Start by working the five round flowers of the central design, each with five gathered ribbons. Then work individual ribbons for the tall background flowers. The template shows their positions, and the photograph shows the distribution of the colours.

Gathered ribbon flowers in the border: Work the ribbon flowers in the colours shown in the photograph.

EMBROIDERY

See Stitching, page 115, for instructions on how to work the stitches.

Daisies: Work the daisies in white Coton Perlé thread, using straight stitches.

French knots: Add French knot centres to the round central flowers using both yellows silks. Work French knots in a matching colour between the single flowers of the tall background flower spikes. Add a single French knot centre in deep yellow to each daisy.

French knot flowers: The small stitched flowers are worked with five deep mauve French knots in a circle with a deep yellow French knot in the centre.

Bullion knot flowers: Work the flowers in both yellows, positioning them as in the photograph.

Foliage: Use two strands of pale green silk to work the small straight stitches along the tall flowers. Keep these stitches at a sharp angle to the imaginary stem and vary the number of stitches in each group. Radiate straight stitches in two strands each of both the greens to form fans at the base of the bouquet.

The border: Fill spaces between the border flowers with daisies, French knot flowers in deep mauve, bullion knot flowers in deeper yellow and fans of straight stitches in both greens to represent the foliage.

FINISHING AND MAKING UP

Place the embroidered fabric over the Vilene. See Presentation, page 121, for instructions on how to mount the work.

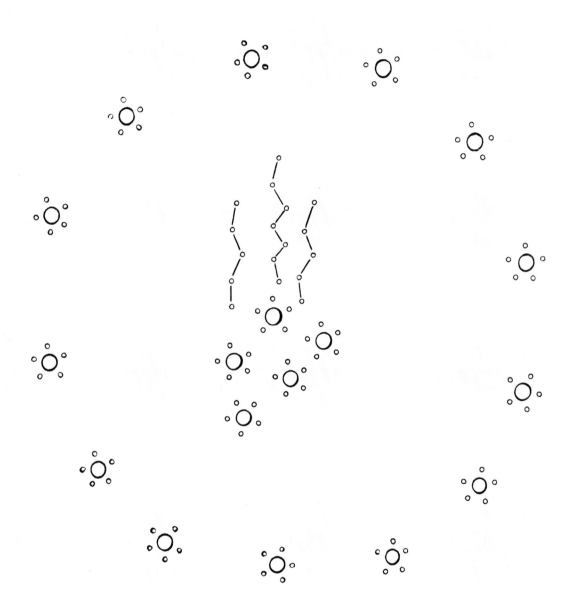

TEMPLATE *for Flower Circle*

STITCH KEY	
○	Round flower with five gathered petals
∘	Single gathered petal for tall flowers

A Child's Special Outfit

WOVEN AND GATHERED RIBBON FLOWERS,
STITCHED RIBBON AND EMBROIDERY

The jewel-like richness of ribbon embroidery transforms an attractive outfit into something special. The pretty scalloped collar on the child's dress is embossed with embroidered flowers, making it fit for a bridesmaid or for any very important occasion. Giving an exceptionally lovely touch to her hair, the band will thrill any little girl, more especially if she wears it with the ribbon embroidered dress. Easy to fit on to a pre-formed band, the roses, daisies, gathered and star shape flowers are all linked by the ferns.

The Dress

The woven roses and the French knot flowers are worked to tone with the rich colour of the fabric of the dress and could be repeated on a pocket or even on the lower edge of the dress.

Materials

• Dress fabric and suitable pattern (STYLE 2436 was used for the dress in the photograph)

OFFRAY EMBROIDERY RIBBON,
ONE CARD EACH OF:
2mm   Daffodil 645
               Yellow gold 660
               Light pink 117
4mm   Colonial rose 168
• Coton Perlé, white, one skein
• Anchor stranded cotton (floss), green 215, one skein
• Coton à Broder, pink 57, one skein

Equipment

• No. 24 tapestry needle for woven ribbon roses
• No. 7 embroidery needle
• Embroidery scissors

PREPARATION

Mark the scallop edge of the collar on to the collar material. Trace the template (page 28) on to tracing paper, then place this underneath the fabric and mark the spokes for the woven ribbon roses and the dots for the centres of both the daisies and ribbon French knot flowers. The template shows the size of the scallop that was used for the collar edge. If your collar has a different size scallop, trace the edge of two scallops and position the design in the centre of each. Then use the tracing to position the design on to the collar fabric.

STITCHING

RIBBON EMBROIDERY

This is done before the garment is made up. See Working with Ribbon, page 11. Refer often to the photograph of the finished piece opposite for positioning the ribbon. Work each group of flowers as follows:

Woven ribbon roses: With pink Coton à Broder, make a foundation wheel with seven spokes. Use the tapestry needle for weaving the 4mm deep pink ribbon, remembering to start off by weaving quite firmly and then slacken off towards the end of the weaving.

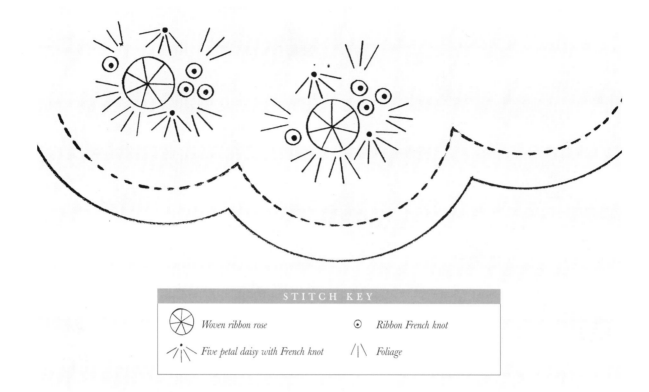

STITCH KEY		
Woven ribbon rose		Ribbon French knot
Five petal daisy with French knot		Foliage

TEMPLATE *for Dress collar*

Daisies: Using the embroidery needle, work the petals in pale pink ribbon, making fans of five straight stitches.
Ribbon French knots: Using the paler yellow ribbon, work five French knots in a circle round the dot to the left of the woven pink rose, and around the two dots to the right hand side of the rose. The third ribbon French knot flower is worked in the deeper yellow. Work a pale yellow French knot for the centre of the deeper yellow flower and a deeper yellow one for the centre of the paler yellow flowers. Ribbon French knots are worked in exactly the same way as the thread ones (see Stitching, page 118).

EMBROIDERY
See Stitching (page 115) for information on how to work the stitches.
Foliage: Using two strands of green stranded cotton (floss), work fans of three straight stitches to represent the foliage and small straight stitches surrounding the flowers.

French knots: Work a French knot in white Coton Perlé thread for the daisy centre. Using two strands of green stranded cotton (floss), place French knots in the spaces between the flowers.

FINISHING AND MAKING UP

The dress is now ready to be made up according to the pattern instructions. When you press the garment, take care that you don't squash the ribbon flowers.

The Alice Band

Choose the colours of the background fabric and the ribbons to match and tone with the colours of the dress, adding that finishing touch to a special outfit.

PREPARATION

To make a pattern to fit the Alice band, take a fine piece of scrap cotton fabric and draw a long line across the centre of it. Lay this line along the centre of the outside

Materials

- Covered, padded Alice band
- Closely woven covering fabric in white, 7 x 19in (18 x 48cm)

OFFRAY DOUBLE-FACE RIBBON, 3MM WIDE:

Shocking pink 175, 2¼yd (2m)

Lemon 640, 39in (1m)

Cream 815, 39in (1m)

OFFRAY EMBROIDERY RIBBON,
ONE CARD EACH OF:

2mm Carnation 095   7mm Tea rose 140

- Offray double-face satin ribbon, 23mm wide, ivory 810, 39in (1m)

DMC COTON À BRODER, ONE SKEIN EACH OF:

White blanc   Green 702

Cream ecru   Pink 602

Yellow 444

- Anchor stranded cotton (floss), pale green 253, one skein

Equipment

- Embroidery frame, 7 x 19in (18 x 48cm)
- No. 24 tapestry needle for weaving the roses
- No. 7 embroidery needle
- Embroidery scissors
- Sharp pencil

edge of the ready-made band and pin along each edge. Draw a pencil line from pin to pin and then remove the pins. This gives an area in which the embroidery must be contained. Cut out this shape ready to use as a pattern.

Stretch the fabric on to the frame and secure with either staples or drawing pins. If you use pins cover the heads with masking tape to stop threads catching on them.

Trace the template (see page 30), lay the tracing under the fabric and mark the flower positions and fern stems with a sharp pencil.

Lay your prepared pattern paper centrally over the transferred design, pin into position and then run a tacking thread round the outside of it – this will define the area needed to cover the headband.

STITCHING

RIBBON EMBROIDERY

See Working with Ribbon, page 11. Follow the template carefully and refer often to the photograph of the finished piece for colour and positioning the ribbon.

Woven ribbon roses: With Coton à Broder to match the ribbon, make nine foundation wheels, each with seven spokes. Use the tapestry needle for weaving the ribbon, remembering to start off quite firmly and then slacken off towards the ends of the weaving. Start with the three central roses, which are pink.

Daisies: Work the petals in 2mm pink embroidery ribbon, making fans of straight stitches.

Gathered ribbon flowers: Work gathered ribbon single petal flowers in the 7mm embroidery ribbon.

EMBROIDERY

See Stitching, page 115, for information on how to work the stitches.

Small star flowers: Work six or seven straight stitches in yellow Coton à Broder.

French knots: Finish each daisy and each gathered ribbon flower with a yellow Coton à Broder French knot.

Foliage: Work the pale green ferns in two strands of pale green Anchor stranded cotton (floss). These are made up from a back stitch stem and small straight stitches which join the stem at sloping angles. Work groups of three fan-shaped short straight stitches in the darker green around the flowers where the spaces allow.

FINISHING AND MAKING UP

Cut out the embroidered area, leaving sufficient fabric round the outside to turn over the headband so that the edges will meet underneath. Starting at one end of the headband, lace the fabric from side to side, ensuring that there are no creases on the right side and continuing to the other end. Use 23mm ribbon to line the headband, pinning it in place and oversewing along each side.

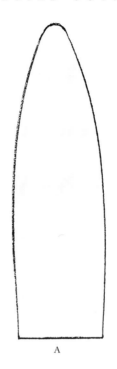

A

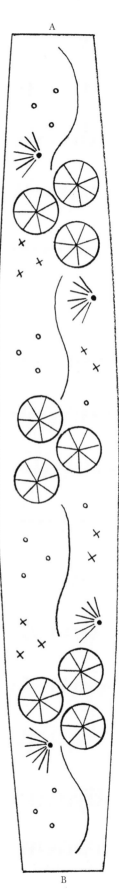

A

B

STITCH KEY

 Woven ribbon rose

 Daisy with French knot

○ *Single gathered petal*

× *Star flower*

(Above) *Detail of ribbon embroidery*
(Right) TEMPLATE *for Alice Band*

B

Heart-shaped Cushion

WOVEN AND GATHERED
RIBBON FLOWERS, EMBROIDERY
AND RIBBON WORK

An exquisite cushion, dainty and so feminine, evocative of the Victorian boudoir and pretty enough to take pride of place in today's bedroom. The cushion's central panel features a delicate tracery of flowers and stems, garlanded with ribbons and all beautifully framed by frills and flounces.

Materials

- Closely-woven cushion fabric in white, two pieces, each 14in (35.5cm) square
- Two pieces of the same fabric for the frill, each 5 x 39in (12.5 cm x 1m)

OFFRAY EMBROIDERY RIBBON,
4MM WIDE, ONE CARD EACH OF:

Mango (deep pink) 244	Buttermilk 824
Tea rose (mid pink) 140	Iris 447
Carnation (pale pink) 095	

- Panda Polyester organdie Wedding-Print ribbon, 35mm wide, silver/white 4636, 39in (1m)

ANCHOR COTON À BRODER,
ONE SKEIN EACH OF:

Yellow 302	Pink 051
Deep green 210	White 001
Mid green 208	

- Madeira metallic No. 12, silver, one reel
- Pregathered lace edging in white, 2¼yd (2m)
- Heart-shaped cushion pad and white cotton fabric to cover

OR

- White cotton fabric to make heart-shaped cover and polyester filling

Equipment

- Embroidery frame 14in (35.5cm) square
- No 24 tapestry needle for woven ribbon roses
- No 7 embroidery needle
- Embroidery scissors
- Tracing paper
- Sharp pencil

First, trace off the heart-shaped design on page 35. Take a large sheet of tracing paper, fold in half and open flat again. Trace off one complete half of the heart shape along the fold. Fold the tracing paper in half again along the original crease and cut out along the traced lines giving you a complete heart shape. Place the heart-shaped pattern onto the fabric. Tack (baste) around the shape for the cushion outline. This is the finished size of the cushion – no allowance has been made for turnings. Trace the template central panel, including the vertical lines on either side of the design. Lay the tracing paper under the fabric and mark out the design in pencil.

PREPARATION

Stretch the cushion fabric tightly on the embroidery frame. Secure with either staples or drawing pins (see page 14). If you use pins cover the heads with masking tape to stop threads catching on them.

STITCHING

RIBBON EMBROIDERY

See Working with Ribbon, page 11. Follow the template carefully and refer often to the photograph of the finished piece for positioning the ribbon.

Woven ribbon roses: With pink Coton à Broder, make nine foundation wheels, each with seven spokes. Place the colours as shown on the finished item. Each group has one rose of each of the three pink ribbons. Use the tapestry needle for weaving the ribbon, remembering to start off by weaving quite firmly and then slacken off towards the end of the weaving.

Mauve flowers: Each mauve flower is made up of five ribbon French knots worked in a circle, and there are three mauve flowers around each group of woven ribbon roses. Ribbon French knots are worked in exactly the same way as the thread ones (see Stitching, page 118). Inside each circle of French knots, work one gathered yellow ribbon.

Tall flowers: Work a series of single yellow petals in gathered ribbons, as shown on the design.

EMBROIDERY

Tall flowers: Work yellow French knots down the stems in Coton à Broder, and finish with short straight stitches in mid green Coton à Broder.

Mauve flowers: Work a French knot in yellow Coton à Broder through the yellow gathered ribbon in the centre and one between each mauve ribbon French knot.

Foliage: Work fans of straight stitches at the base of the tall flowers with green Coton à Broder to represent the leaves. Finish off the design with fans of deep green stitches around and between the roses.

Bow and trails: Outline in back stitch, using doubled silver metallic thread. To complete, work chain stitch in white Coton à Broder down the centre.

RIBBON WORK

Organdie patterned ribbon and pregathered lace edging: Lay white lace edging up to the vertical lines each side of the design and tack (baste) into position. Then lay the wedding print ribbon over the lace edging and attach with white French knots in white Coton à Broder. Make sure the wedding print ribbon is lying flat, then place lace edging under the unattached side. Attach with French knots in white Coton à Broder.

FINISHING AND MAKING UP

Lay the pregathered lace edging on to the line at the edge of the cushion shape and tack (baste). To make the frill, take the two pieces of white cushion fabric measuring 5 x 39in (12.5cm x 1m) and join at both ends. Press the seam open. Fold in half with the right sides outside. Gather the frill and tack (baste) into place with the right side to the right side of the cushion cover.

Cut out the backing fabric using the heart-shaped template, allowing ⅜in (1cm) turnings. Place the right side to the embroidered front, tack (baste) and stitch, leaving about a 6in (15cm) opening to turn the cushion cover. Tack (baste) and stitch either by hand or machine. Turn the cushion cover to the right side.

Cover the heart-shaped cushion pad with white cotton fabric. If you are unable to obtain such a pad, use the heart-shaped pattern to cut two pieces of white cotton fabric, allowing for a narrow seam; stitch these, right sides together, along the pattern line leaving a small opening. Turn out and fill with polyester filling to obtain a good, firm heart shape. Stitch up the opening.

Insert the cushion pad into the finished cushion and stitch up the opening as neatly as possible.

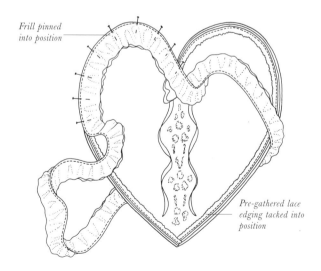

Frill pinned into position

Pre-gathered lace edging tacked into position

FIGURE 1 *Making the cover*

Detail of ribbon embroidery

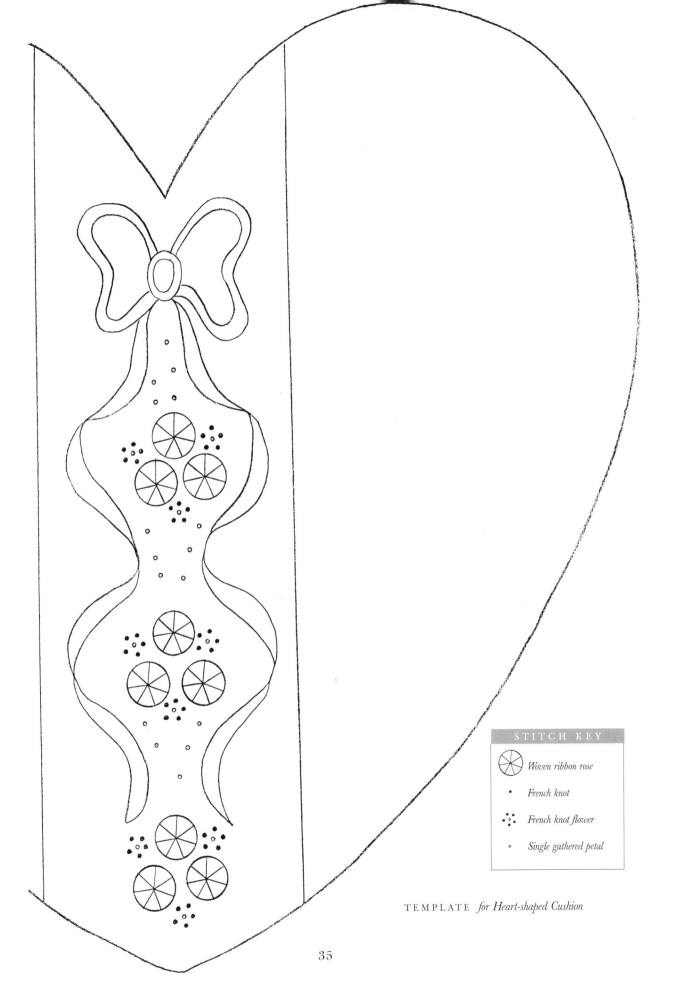

STITCH KEY

Woven ribbon rose

French knot

French knot flower

Single gathered petal

TEMPLATE *for Heart-shaped Cushion*

35

Heart of Roses Greetings Card

WOVEN AND GATHERED RIBBON FLOWERS
WITH EMBROIDERY

What better way to express your feelings to someone special than to embroider and send this gorgeous little card? Groups of glorious pink roses dominate the heart-shaped design, linked by mauve flowered stems, interspersed with delicate creamy French knots and set off with dainty foliage in ribbons and threads. The garland knot in pink cross-stitch is outlined in silver to add a touch of sparkle. Quick and easy to do, this card will bring endless pleasure.

Materials

- Charles Craft 14-count fabric in cream, 8in (20cm) square

OFFRAY EMBROIDERY RIBBON,
4MM WIDE, ONE CARD EACH OF:
    Iris (mauve) 447
    Tea rose (medium pink) 140
    Mango (deep pink) 244
    Moonstone (pale pink) 203
    Forest (green) 587

ANCHOR COTON À BRODER,
ONE SKEIN EACH OF:
    Pale yellow 301   Pink 970
    Pale green 265   Mauve 108

- Small piece of Vilene extra heavy interfacing ³⁄₈in (1cm) larger all round than the aperture of your card
- Kreinik silver cord 001C, one reel
- Card with heart-shaped aperture

Equipment

- Embroidery frame, 5½ x 3½in (14 x 9cm) or 6in (15cm) circular
- No. 24 tapestry needle for the cross stitch, back stitch and woven ribbon roses
- No. 7 embroidery needle for gathered ribbon flowers
- Embroidery scissors

PREPARATION

Stretch the fabric tightly in the circular frame or attach it to the rectangular frame with staples or drawing pins (see pages 14 and 16). If you use pins cover the heads with masking tape to stop threads catching on them. Mark the size of the heart-shaped aperture centrally on your fabric using a light thread.

STITCHING

EMBROIDERY

See Stitching, page 115, for instructions on how to work the stitches.

Cross stitch: Using a single thread of Coton à Broder, follow the chart and work the pink bow and the green stems. Outline the bow in back stitch, in silver metallic thread using it double.

Feathery foliage: Using a single thread of green Coton à Broder, work the side stems in back stitch, making each stitch approximately the length of two squares of the fabric. Then add small straight stitches at either side of the stem – two for each back stitch at a 45° degree angle to the stem.

RIBBON EMBROIDERY

See Working with Ribbon, page 11. Follow the chart below carefully and refer often to the detail photograph left for positioning the ribbon.

Gathered ribbon flowers: Work five gathered ribbon flowers in mauve on each main stem. Dot mauve French knots along the stem, and add groups of pale yellow French knots, using Coton à Broder doubled.

Woven ribbon roses: With pale yellow Coton à Broder, make nine foundation wheels, each with seven spokes. Use the tapestry needle for weaving the ribbon, remembering to start off by weaving quite firmly and then slacken off towards the end of the weaving.

Leaves: Using the green ribbon in the embroidery needle, make straight stitches in groups around the roses.

FINISHING AND MAKING UP

See Presentation, page 121, for instructions on how to make up the card.

Detail of ribbon embroidery

CHART *for Heart of Roses*

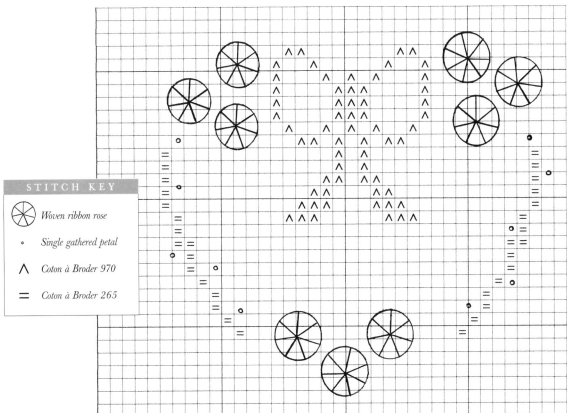

STITCH KEY

⊛ Woven ribbon rose

∘ Single gathered petal

∧ Coton à Broder 970

= Coton à Broder 265

Christening Gown

*Panels of ribbon embroidery, each edged with lace,
turn this simple christening gown into a treasured
heirloom of the future. With the simple elegance of the
white ribbon flowers on white cotton, daintily worked,
this gown will surely be passed from generation
to generation for years to come.*

*The christening robe in the photograph was made
using Style Pattern No. 2436 in the smallest size. A
suitable pattern with a central skirt panel could not
be found, so a 8¼in (21cm) wide panel was cut from
the centre of the front skirt and replaced by the
embroidered piece. The panel has alternating
embroidered and plain sections, which are divided by
pregathered lace. The material used was fine cotton
but cotton lawn would be equally successful.*

Materials

- Fabric requirements will depend on the pattern you
  chose, plus a small amount extra to allow for the
  central panel and turnings
- Pregathered lace for the central panel 3¾yd (3.5m)
- Anchor stranded cotton (floss), one skein of white
- Anchor Coton à Broder, one skein of white
- Offray Embroidery Ribbon, 4mm, antique white
  028, two cards
- Indian rayon thread, white, one reel

*The Christening Gown and two Christening Cards, For a Boy
(see page 42) and For a Girl (page 44)*

Equipment

- Embroidery frame: the four embroidered panels in the photograph were worked together on a rectangular frame, measuring 22 x 10in (56 x 25cm) and cut apart afterwards. Each panel could be worked separately on a 10in (25.5cm) circular frame, which would mean allowing a little extra fabric
- No. 24 tapestry needle for woven ribbon roses
- No. 7 embroidery needle
- Tracing paper
- Sharp pencil

PREPARATION

Trace the template and transfer the design to the fabric carefully marking out the ribbon shapes and the dots to show the centre point of the ribbon roses.

Stretch the fabric tightly in the circular frame or attach it to the rectangular frame with staples or drawing pins (see pages 14 and 16). If you use pins cover the heads with masking tape to stop threads catching on them.

Work the full design on the panels for the skirt. For the front yoke of the dress, use just the centre of the design as indicated on the template.

STITCHING

EMBROIDERY

See Stitching, page 115, for instructions on how to work the stitches.

Ribbon shapes: Outline the ribbon shapes in back stitch using two strands of Anchor stranded cotton (floss). Work chain stitch along the centre of each of the ribbon shapes, using a double thread of the Indian rayon. Remember that, when you are using multiple threads, it is better to try to avoid having ends close to the eye of the needle.

RIBBON EMBROIDERY

See Working with Ribbon, page 11. Follow the template carefully and refer often to the detail photograph

TEMPLATE *for Christening Gown panel*

below and on pages 38–39 for positioning the ribbon.

Woven ribbon roses: With Coton à Broder, make five foundation wheels in each panel, each with seven spokes. Use the tapestry needle for weaving the ribbon, remembering to start off by weaving quite firmly and then slacken off towards the end of the weaving.

Gathered ribbon flowers: Following the template, work five single gathered flowers on each side of the design.

EMBROIDERY

Daisies: Using Coton à Broder, work each daisy as a fan of seven straight stitches.

Foliage: Work small fans of three or four straight stitches around each of the groups of flowers. Use two strands of Anchor stranded cotton (floss).

French knots: Finish each daisy with a white French knot centre. Work a French knot in the centre of each gathered ribbon flower.

FINISHING AND MAKING UP

Cut out each of the embroidered panels to measure $8^{5}/_{8}$ x $5^{1}/_{8}$in (22 x 13cm). Each of the four finished panels will be $4^{1}/_{4}$in (11cm) deep, so take the 17in (44cm) from the total measurement for the length of the central skirt panel to find the depth of each of the four plain panels. In the example, the skirt was 30in (76cm) from waist to hem, so each plain panel was $3^{1}/_{8}$in (8cm) deep; cut each one 4in (10cm) deep to allow for turnings.

Sew the embroidered and plain panels together alternately, sandwiching a length of pregathered lace between each section. Set the whole panel into the centre of the front skirt, again with lace edging. When gathering the waist of the skirt, put more of the fullness into the two sides, leaving the front panel smoother.

Detail of ribbon embroidery

Christening Cards

These cross stitch cards make perfect presents for the proud parents and permanent mementoes of the birth of a baby. Special enough to frame, the pictures are delightful birth samplers and, with pride of place on the nursery wall, will become well-loved, an indelible part of magical childhood memories. With separate designs for a girl and boy and a full alphabet, you will be able to make each card special with the appropriate name and date.

For a Boy card

For a Boy

EMBROIDERY, RIBBON WORK AND SEQUINS

The card to welcome a baby boy has a military flavour. Satin and Kreinik ribbon have been used with brightly coloured threads to work the border, soldier, drum and trumpet with its banner to state the date of birth.

Materials

- Evenweave fabric 14-count in the colour of your choice, 6 x 8½in (15 x 21.5cm)

  OFFRAY DOUBLE-FACE SATIN RIBBON, 3MM, 39IN (1M) EACH OF:

  Red 252   Blue 352
- Kreinik Balger metallic ribbon ⅛in wide, gold 002, one reel

  DMC STRANDED COTTON (FLOSS):

  Red 46   Brown 436

  Blue 142   Yellow 302

  Black 403   White 1
- Madeira metallic No. 12, gold 33, one reel
- Fifteen small gold sequins
- Card with 4 x 5½in (10 x 14cm) aperture
- Vilene extra heavy interfacing, 4 x 5½in (10 cm x 14 cm)

Equipment

- Embroidery frame 6 x 8½in (15 x 21.5cm)
- No. 24 tapestry needle
- No. 7 embroidery needle for adding the sequins
- Embroidery scissors

PREPARATION

Attach the fabric tightly frame or attach to the rectangular frame with staples or drawing pins (see pages 14 and 16). If you use pins cover the heads with masking tape to stop threads catching on them. Mark the centre of the fabric both horizontally and vertically with a light thread. Mark the size of the aperture of the card also with a light thread.

Refer to the photograph opposite and mark with pins the position for the two rows of ribbon used as the border. Couch the two coloured ribbons using two strands of the matching threads and making a stitch every three squares (see Stitching, page 119).

STITCHING

CROSS STITCH

See Stitching, page 115, for instructions on how to work the stitches.

If the boy's name is long, start the soldier and drum three squares lower than shown.

Using two strands of thread, follow the chart and work the cross stitch design. For the grey thread on the top of the drum and the bottom of the soldier's hat, use one strand of black and one strand of white thread together in your needle. Remember that the top stitch of each cross must lie in the same direction to give a neat, even finish.

The name: This is worked across the top, leaving a gap of one square of fabric between the top of the trumpet and the base of the first letter. Leave one square between each letter. Work the name in cross stitch, referring to the letter chart (page 47).

RIBBON EMBROIDERY

See Working with Ribbon, page 11.

Thread the Kreinik gold ribbon into the tapestry needle and stitch the belt, two cuffs, rope work on the drum and the outline of the banner in straight stitches as indicated on the chart.

EMBROIDERY

See Stitching, page 115, for instructions on how to work the stitches.

The date: In back stitch, work the date, month and year using lower case letters and numerals (chart, page 47) and position as in the worked design.

The banner: Using the metallic thread, catch the edges of the banner with French knots worked about every centimetre. Stitch the tassels on the base and top of the banner with four straight stitches caught together at the top.

The soldier: Using metallic thread double, work straight stitches for the hat plume and cross stitches for the epaulets.

Outlines: Using the metallic thread double, back stitch down the outside of the soldier's legs and outline the trumpet and the lettering.

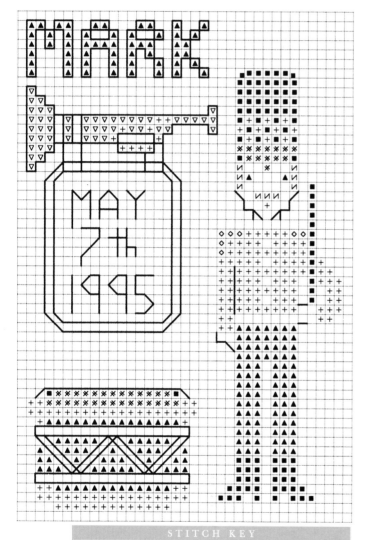

SEQUINS

With the metallic thread, come up through the fabric where each sequin is to be placed and thread on the sequin. Work a French knot and take the needle back down through the sequin. There are seven sequins on the drum, four on the jacket to represent buttons and one in each corner of the ribbon border.

FINISHING AND MAKING UP

Press any areas of the background fabric that you can reach without going over the ribbon. See Presentation, page 121, for instructions on how to make up the card.

For a Girl

GATHERED RIBBON FLOWERS, EMBROIDERY AND BEADING

This charming birth sampler shows how ribbon embroidery can enhance a traditional cross stitch project.

Materials

- Charles Craft 14-count fabric in antique white, 9¾in (25cm) square

SILK RIBBON, 3MM WIDE,
19¾IN (50CM) EACH OF:

Deep pink   Buttercup yellow
Pale pink   Cream
Lilac

- Madeira metallic No. 12, gold 33, one reel

ANCHOR COTON À BRODER,
ONE SKEIN EACH OF:

Cream 926   Lilac 108
Light brown 388   Yellow 301
Pinks 50 and 57   White
Greens 260 and 262

- Beadesign beads, one packet each of: cream 45 and yellow 48
- Card with an aperture of approximately 5½ x 3¾in (14 x 9.5cm), landscape
- Small piece of Vilene extra heavy interfacing, ¾in (1cm) larger all round than the aperture of your card

STITCH KEY

■	DMC 403 Black	▽	DMC 302 Yellow
◇	Madeira metallic No. 12 Gold 33	✕	DMC 403 Black + DMC 1 White
▲	DMC 142 Blue	И	DMC 436 Brown
+	DMC 46 Red		

Equipment

- Embroidery frame, 8 x 6in (20 x 15cm) or 8in (20cm) circular
- Embroidery scissors
- No. 24 tapestry needle for the cross stitch
- No. 7 embroidery needle for the ribbon work
- Beading needle

PREPARATION

Stretch the fabric tightly in the circular frame or attach it to the rectangular frame with staples or drawing pins (see pages 14 and 16). If you use pins cover the heads with masking tape to stop threads catching on them. Mark the centre of the fabric both horizontally and vertically with a light thread. Mark the size of the aperture of the card also with a light thread to help you position the embroidered design.

For a Girl card

STITCHING

CROSS STITCH

See Stitching, page 115, for instructions on how to work the stitches.

Using a single thread of Coton à Broder, follow the chart on page 46 and stitch the rabbit, the harness and the cart outline. Remember that the top stitch of each cross must always lie in the same direction. Each cross is worked over one square of the fabric.

The name: This is worked across the top, leaving a gap of two squares of fabric between the top of the cart and the base of the letters. For a short name, the letters can have three squares in between them but, for a longer name, leave only two squares. Work the name in cross stitch, referring to the letter chart on page 47.

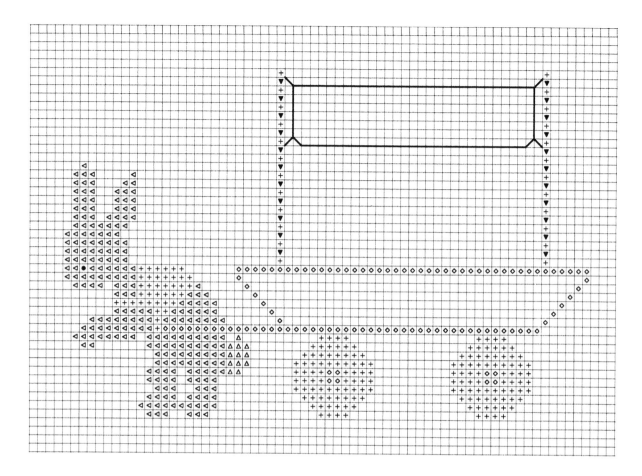

The date: In back stitch, work the date, month and year using the lower case letters and numerals on the chart opposite and position as in the worked design.

The cart: Work the basket-work infill for the cart in wide cross stitch, with each cross going over one square in depth but two in width. Use the two pink shades of Coton à Broder alternately.

The tassels: Use the gold thread doubled for the tassels. Work four straight stitches and then overstitch near the top with two stitches, drawing the top of the four threads together.

Back stitch: Outline the rabbit in light brown. Outline the harness and the name in double gold. Underline the date in double gold. Back stitch around the date and underlining to form the cart's banner.

Grass: Work the grass in straight stitches grouped together, using first the light green and then add the darker shade.

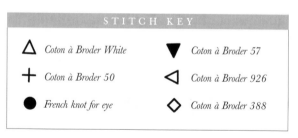

STITCH KEY		
△ Coton à Broder White		▼ Coton à Broder 57
+ Coton à Broder 50		◁ Coton à Broder 926
● French knot for eye		◇ Coton à Broder 388

RIBBON EMBROIDERY

See Working with Ribbon, page 11. Refer often to the photograph of the finished card on page 45 for colour and positioning the ribbon.

Gathered ribbon flowers: Place single yellow and cream ribbons among the straight stitches of the grass. In the cart, place three round flowers, each worked with five pieces of pink ribbon. Work lilac ribbons to represent tall flowers, and place single cream and yellow ribbons between them.

BEADING

See Stitching, page 115. Using the beading needle, stitch a single yellow bead in the centre of each of the cream and yellow flowers. Fill the centres of the large pink round flowers with cream beads and yellow French knots.

EMBROIDERY

French knots: Work a French knot in pink for the rabbit's eye. Work French knots in the centres of the three large pink round flowers. Add French knots to the lilac flowers – two or three above the top ribbon and then along the sides of the three ribbons. To help give a three-dimensional effect, work lilac French knots as in the original design.

Foliage: Work small straight green stitches along the tall flowers and in groups of three around the other flowers.

FINISHING AND MAKING UP

Press any areas of the background fabric that you can reach without going over the ribbon. See Presentation, page 121, for instructions on how to make up the card.

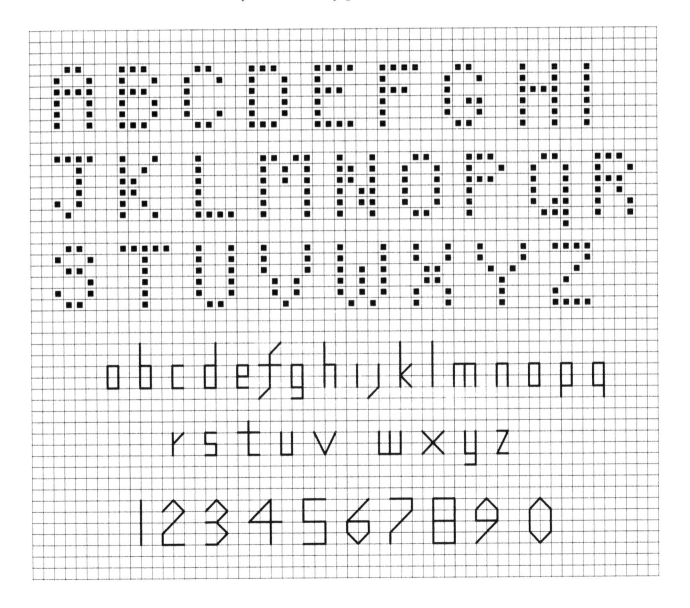

Oval Mauves

GATHERED RIBBON FLOWERS, EMBROIDERY AND QUILTING

The deep mauve ribbon flowers provide the focal point of this picture, gradually fading to the paler mauves above. The dramatic curves of the white flowered stems emphasise the design shape and form a framework for the yellow spikes and pale yellow sprays. A final touch of elegance is provided by the quilted background.

Materials

- Cotton fabric in pale green, 10in (25.5cm) square

ANCHOR STRANDED COTTON (FLOSS),
ONE SKEIN EACH OF:

Medium mauve 111	Pale green 260
Pale mauve 108	Deep yellow 301
Deep green 262	Pale yellow 300
Medium green 261	White 002

PANDA DOUBLE SATIN RIBBON, 3MM WIDE:

Medium mauve 262	1yd (92cm)
Pale mauve 252	27in (69cm)
Deep yellow 070	27in (69cm)
Pale yellow 345	15in (38cm)
White 235	27in (69cm)

- Vilene extra heavy interfacing, 7 x 5½in (18 x 14cm)
- Double mount with oval aperture, 6 x 4½in (15 x 11.5cm)

Equipment

- Embroidery frame, 8in (20cm) circular
- No. 7 embroidery needle
- Embroidery scissors
- Soft pencil

PREPARATION

Stretch the fabric on to the embroidery frame (see page 16). Trace the template and transfer the design to the fabric. Using a soft pencil, mark the dots which show where the ribbons are to be placed, the outlines of the leaves, the daisy centres and the central vein of the ferns.

The lines of the tall spiked flowers, the petals of the daisies and the ferns are drawn in to suggest the position of the stitches so do not need to be marked on the fabric.

STITCHING

RIBBON EMBROIDERY

See Working with Ribbon, page 11. Follow the template carefully and refer often to the photograph of the finished piece for positioning the ribbon.

Gathered ribbon flowers: Work the three deeper mauve flowers, followed by the three pale mauve flowers. Place the single gathered ribbon petals for the yellow and white tall flowers.

EMBROIDERY

See Stitching (page 115) for information on how to work the stitches. Use six strands of thread for all French knots, three strands for the white daisy petals and two strands for the remainder of the embroidery.

Oval flowers: To suggest the flat outside petals, work each petal in three straight stitches of medium mauve thread referring to the photograph opposite. Fill the flower centres with French knots in pale mauve.

Round flowers: Work the centres in deep yellow French knots.

Daisies: Work three French knots in deep yellow for each daisy centre. Work the petals in white with straight stitches radiating out from the centre.

Tall flowers: Using the appropriate colour to match the ribbon flowers, work French knots along the line of the tall spiked flowers. Complete these flowers with small straight stitches in pale green.

Ferns: Use pale green to work the central vein of the ferns in back stitch and the straight stitches on each side.

Large leaves and stems: Outline the large leaves and any stems in medium green backstitch. Fill in the leaves with straight stitches in deep green – refer to the photograph opposite for the direction of the stitches. Add a few straight stitches of deep green among the central flowers to give your picture depth.

FINISHING AND MAKING UP

Cut out the Vilene to the size shown on the template. Place the embroidery on the Vilene, right side up. Attach the Vilene by hand with small running stitches or by machine, stitching all the way round the design as shown on the template.

Quilt through both layers, by hand or machine, following the lines shown in the photograph.

Mount the work on to a piece of card (see page 121).

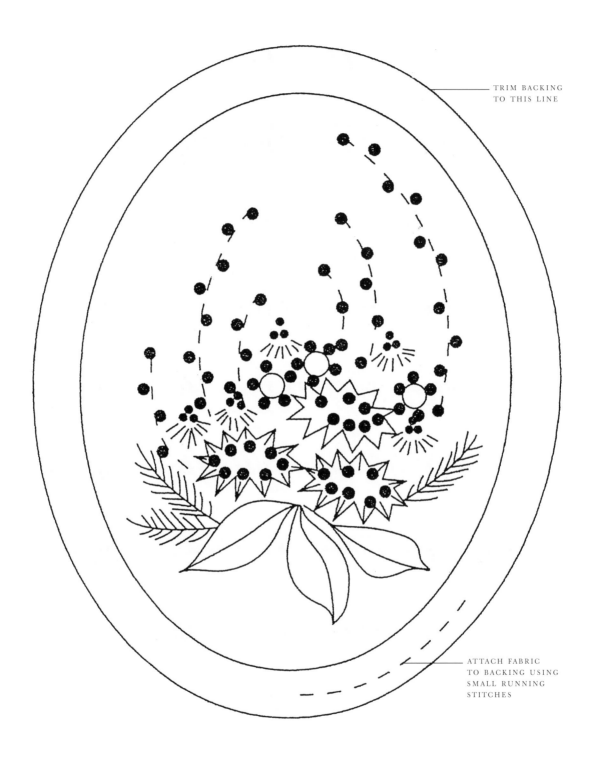

TRIM BACKING
TO THIS LINE

ATTACH FABRIC
TO BACKING USING
SMALL RUNNING
STITCHES

TEMPLATE *for Oval Mauves*

Ribbon Embroidered Boxes

*Ribbon embroidery looks particularly lovely applied to boxes. Make your own box,
as we have with the Small Square Box or cover and decorate a ready-made box,
such as the Ribboned Etui. Choose the materials for your box carefully – let the
patterned fabric you use be an inspiration for your embroidery, dictating
colours and form. Make the outer covering and the lining fabrics tone or contrast.*

Small Square Box

BOX WITH RIBBON EMBROIDERED
AND BEADED LID

Materials
(chosen to match the fabrics used for the box and lining)

OFFRAY DOUBLE-FACE SATIN RIBBON,
3MM WIDE:

Mauve 436, 29½in (0.75m) Lilac mist 420, 20in(0.5m)
Iris 447, 20in (0.5m)   New coral 116, 78in (2m)

ANCHOR COTON À BRODER,
ONE SKEIN EACH OF:

Deeper yellow 305   Deeper green 267
Paler yellow 301   Paler green 208
Pink 028

- Beadesign beads, one packet each of gold 71 and green 37
- DMC No. 5 perlé, white, one skein
- A piece of the outer covering fabric used for the box, 9⅓in (25cm) square

FOR THE BOX

- Greyboard or similar, 2mm thick
- Thin card (e.g. cereal packaging) for lining
- Lining fabric, approximately 9¾in (25cm)
- Felt, thin wadding or similar, for padding
- Outer covering fabric, approximately 9¾in (25cm)
- Strong thread for lacing
- Sewing thread to match the fabric

Equipment

- Embroidery frame, 8in (20cm) circular
- No. 24 tapestry needle for the woven ribbon roses
- No. 7 embroidery needle for the gathered flowers and the embroidery
- Beading needle
- Embroidery scissors
- Tracing paper
- Sharp pencil

FOR MAKING THE BOX

- Stanley or craft knife
- Metal rule
- Cutting surface
- Usual sewing items
- Curved needle
- Pencil and ruler
- Set square or right angle

PREPARATION

Stretch the fabric tightly on to the frame (see page 16). Trace the template for the design and outline (page 55). Cut out the outline shape and lay it on the right side of the fabric in the centre. Tack (baste) around the outline. With a large needle, make a hole in the tracing where each ribbon is to be placed and also the centre point of the spokes for the woven roses. Place this over the fabric and, with a sharp pencil, mark dots on to the fabric through the holes in the tracing paper.

STITCHING

RIBBON EMBROIDERY

See Working with Ribbon, page 11. Follow the template carefully and refer often to the detail photograph on page 55 for positioning the ribbon.

Gathered ribbon flowers: With the deepest shade of your main colour, work three gathered ribbon flowers in the spaces 1, 2 and 3. Use the next shade for flowers 4 and 5 and, finally, the palest shade for 6 and 7.

Woven ribbon roses: With the pink Coton à Broder, make seven foundation wheels, each with seven spokes, placing them as shown on the design sheet. Use the tapestry needle for weaving the ribbon of a contrasting colour, remembering to start off by weaving quite firmly and then slacken off towards the end of the weaving.

EMBROIDERY

See Stitching (page 115) for information on how to work the stitches.

Tiny French knots flowers: For each flower, work five yellow French knots in a circle and place a contrasting knot in the centre of each group.

White daisies: Work fans of about seven straight stitches in cotton perlé. The position for these small flowers are not marked on the design sheet as it is easier for you to place them around the design where the spaces permit.

French knots: Fill the centres of the gathered ribbon flowers with French knots in both yellow threads. Work groups of three French knots in pale mauve in empty spaces throughout the design, then fill the whole area with French knots using green threads.

BEADING

See Stitching, page 115. Using the beading needle, stitch a small gold bead into the centre of each white daisy. Add green beads where the spaces allow.

IMPORTANT: Do not take threads across the back of the work between the scallops, as these may show when the fabric is laced over the box lid.

BOX CONSTRUCTION

From thick card, cut: one piece $5\frac{1}{4}$in (13.5cm) square for the internal base; four pieces $5\frac{1}{4}$ x $2\frac{3}{4}$in (13.5 x 7cm) for the base sides; two pieces 6in (15cm) square for the platform base and lid. From thin card, cut one piece $5\frac{1}{8}$in (13cm) square.

It is very important that all measurements are precise and that the card is cut accurately. Rule out and mark accurately in pencil the dimensions on the thick card (2mm thick greyboard or similar), using a set square to ensure that all the corners are right angles (90°). Always check the dimensions carefully before starting to cut the card.

CUTTING THE CARD

Always cut on a cutting mat or special board. Cut the card carefully along the pencil lines using a Stanley knife, or similar craft knife, held against a metal rule. Position the edge of the metal rule on the pencil line and, holding the knife against it, draw the blade steadily towards you with a firm but gentle pressure, repeating the stroke until the card is cut through. Don't cut with the length of the blade – use the point. The indentation made by the pencil will provide a groove which will help to keep the knife in position on the first stroke and, thereafter, the blade will follow the previous cut if you maintain steady pressure.

As each piece of card is cut, mark the dimensions on it in pencil – this is a good practice as, when you go on to make other boxes, it will avoid the pieces becoming confused!

BASE AND SIDES

Cut pieces of lining fabric approximately $\frac{3}{4}$in (2cm) larger all round than each piece of card: one piece $6\frac{3}{4}$in (17.5cm) square, and four pieces $6\frac{3}{4}$ x $4\frac{1}{4}$in (17.5 x 11cm).

Lace each lining piece tightly over the corresponding piece of card, mitring the corners carefully for a smooth unwrinkled surface on the covered/unlaced side. Use strong thread or crochet cotton for lacing. Pin the fabric

and lace one pair of opposite sides, mitre the corners and pin and lace the fabric on the other pair of sides (see Presentation, page 120-121, for lacing instructions and mitring methods).

MAKING BOX BASE

Place one covered side face-to-face with one side of the covered base and sew the edges together through the fabric (see fig. 1).

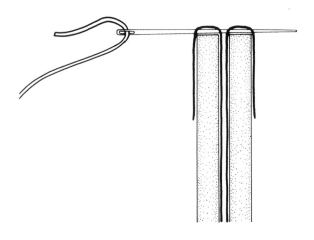

FIGURE 1
Placing fabric-covered card face to face for stitching

Repeat with the remaining sides of the box, attaching each piece to the base before stitching each pair of sides together to form the corners to give a firm neat box base.

PADDING THE BASE

Cut the padding material (felt, thin wadding or suitable alternative) to the exact depth of the box base, 2¾in (7cm), and long enough to fit around the base with the ends butting together. Stitch the butted edges of the padding together so that the seam is flat and the padding is a smooth fit; it may be easier to remove the padding from the base for this purpose and also it helps to avoid accidentally attaching the padding to the side of the box! If additional padding is required, cut a second piece of padding and stitch in the same way to fit over the first.

OUTER COVER

With the padding in place around the base, cut a strip of outer covering fabric approximately 2in (5cm) wider than the depth of the box and long enough to wrap around the sides of the box with an overlap.

With the right side of the fabric against the padding of the box, position the fabric around the base and pin the ends of the fabric closely together over the padding.

Ease the material off the box and re-pin ⅛in (3mm) **inside** the original position, thus making the cover slightly smaller than before. Machine or hand-stitch along this new line. Press the seam open.

COVERING THE BASE OF THE BOX

Remove the padding from the base of the box. Take the prepared outer covering and stand it the right way up inside the box, right side out, positioning the join at a back corner.

Fold the cover over the top edge of the box so that approximately 1in (2.5cm) extends down the outside of the box, and pin into place along the top edge of the box (see fig. 2). Depending on the type of fabric you use and the type of padding you've chosen, it may be necessary to 'ease' the material to lose any slight surplus.

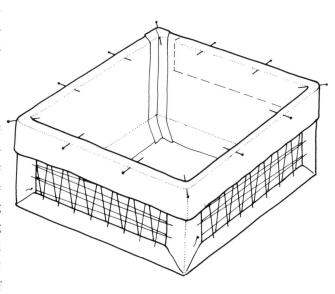

FIGURE 2 *Outer cover ready for stitching*

Detail of ribbon embroidery

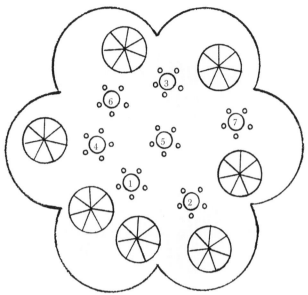

STITCH KEY	
⊕	*Woven ribbon rose*
°O°	*Round flower with five gathered petals*

TEMPLATE *for Small Square Box*

With a sewing thread chosen to match or tone with the lining and outer fabric or both, sew the outer cover to the base along the top outer edge with small even stitches (see fig. 3), being careful just to catch the lining material underneath. (Peep underneath occasionally to check that this is being achieved.)

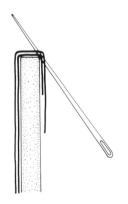

FIGURE 3 *Angle of needle when stitching cover in place*

Remove all pins from the base before replacing the padding and turning the cover out over the padding to the outside of the box, pulling the covering fabric down over the padding and taking care not to move or wrinkle

the padding in the process. Pull the material to the underside of the box (checking that it is pulled evenly) and pin into position. If necessary, smooth out any wrinkles in the padding before pinning the fabric.

Lace the covering fabric underneath the box, first one pair of opposite sides, mitring the corners neatly before lacing the second pair of sides, giving as flat a finish as possible on the undersurface.

MAKING THE BASE PLATFORM

Take one of the pieces of thick card 6in (15cm) square. Cut a piece of outer covering fabric 7½in (19cm) square. Lace the card with fabric as before and place this, lace-side uppermost, on a firm surface. Position the box centrally on this card, pinning it firmly in place, and stitch the lower edge of the box to the fabric covering the base platform, using a curved needle.

LID

Using the remaining piece of card 6in (15cm) square, cut a piece of thick felt or wadding to the same dimensions; use as many layers as you need to achieve the result you want.

Place the embroidered lid fabric, wrong-side uppermost, on a surface (resting on a piece of thick foam will avoid crushing the embroidery) and position the felt and then the card on top.

Pull and pin the outer fabric over the card and lace it firmly, making sure that all lacing stitching are at least $^3/_4$in (2cm) from the edges, so that these stitches will not show after the lid lining is in position. Mitre carefully as these mitres will show.

Take the thin piece of card 5$^1/_8$in (13cm) square, lace over it a piece of lining fabric 6in (15cm) square, making sure any printing on this card does not show through the fabric. Position the lining card centrally over the lacing on the lid and pin firmly into position. Stitch the lining to the lid, using the curved needle.

Detail of ribbon embroidery for the
Ribboned Etui

A Ribboned Etui

GATHERED FLOWERS WITH EMBROIDERY AND BEADING

Try buying ready-made boxes and creating your own unique design to apply to lid or sides. Our design is applied to an etui, an ingeniously constructed box that opens out to reveal a number of compartments. If you decide to make your own etui, you can buy kits by mail order. See Suppliers and Stockists, page 126.

Materials
(chosen to match the fabrics of the box)

- A piece of the box lining fabric 10in (25.5cm) square

  OFFRAY DOUBLE-FACE SATIN RIBBON, 3MM WIDE, 1M EACH OF:
  Iris (deeper mauve) 447   Lemon 640
  Lilac mist (paler mauve) 420

  ANCHOR COTON À BRODER, ONE SKEIN EACH OF:
  Deeper yellow 305   Pink 057
  Paler yellow 386   Green 267

- Coton Perlé No. 5, white, one skein

  BEADESIGN BEADS, ONE PACKET EACH OF:
  Turquoise 21 Pale yellow 48
  Gold 72

Equipment

- Embroidery frame, 6in (15cm) circular
- No. 7 embroidery needle
- Beading needle
- Embroidery scissors
- Sharp pencil
- Tracing paper

PREPARATION

Stretch the fabric tightly into the frame (see page 14). Trace the template opposite and transfer the design to the fabric following the instructions on page 16. Once the marked single gathered petals, gathered ribbon flowers and foliage stems have been embroidered, you will see where the gaps are to place the pink daisy flowers and the white French knot flowers.

STITCHING

RIBBON EMBROIDERY

See Working with Ribbon, page 11. Follow the template carefully and refer often to the detail photograph opposite for positioning the ribbon.

Gathered ribbon flowers: Work the three deeper mauve round flowers followed by the two paler mauve ones.

Yellow spiked flowers: The lines of three dots on the chart indicate the yellow spiked ribbon flowers; work a single gathered ribbon petal for each dot.

EMBROIDERY

French knots: Fill the centres of the round flowers with French knots in both of the yellows. Use the paler yellow Coton à Broder to work the French knots along the line of the three yellow gathered ribbons.

Foliage: Work small straight stitches in green thread to finish off the yellow flower spikes. Back stitch along the marked line of the flower stem in green, and then add the straight stitches along the stem. Keep these stitches at a sharp angle to the stem.

IMPORTANT: Do not take threads across the back of the work between the stems, as these may show when the fabric is laced over a box lid.

Pink daisies: Stitch seven straight stitches, in pink, for each flower.

Tiny French knot flowers: For each flower, work five white French knots in a circle. Fit in both the daisy flowers and the white French knot flowers where the spaces allow.

BEADING

See Stitching, page 115. Using the beading needle, stitch a small gold bead into the centre of each pink flower, and a pale yellow bead in the centre of each white French knot flower. Add pale turquoise beads, again where the spaces allow.

FINISHING AND MAKING UP

Remove the embroidered fabric from the frame, and pad and lace this over a piece of thin card cut to the shape of the top of the box. Using a curved needle, stitch this firmly to the lid of the box, so that it lies flush with the top edge of the sides of the lid.

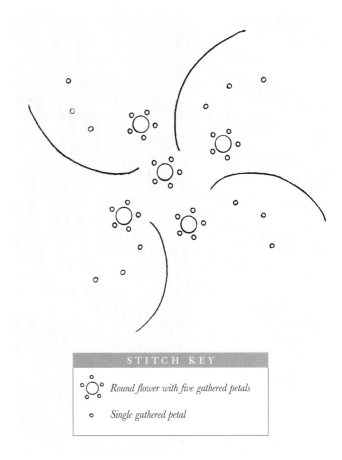

STITCH KEY	
° ⦿ °	*Round flower with five gathered petals*
°	*Single gathered petal*

TEMPLATE *for Ribboned Etui*

'S' for Susan

WOVEN FLOWERS, EMBROIDERY AND BEADING

Personalise all your cards whatever the message – birthday, thank-you, congratulations and more – by embroidering this strong yet simple initial letter design. The chosen initial is outlined in cross stitch and then massed with roses, daisies, French knots and beads to give a really dramatic effect to gladden the eye.

Materials

- Charles Craft 14-count fabric colour Fidler's Life, 8in (20cm) square
- Madeira metallic No. 12, gold 331, one reel

ANCHOR COTON À BRODER,
ONE SKEIN EACH:

Pale yellow 301   Deeper green 267
Pale green 265

- DMC No. 5 perlé, white, one skein

OFFRAY DOUBLE-FACE SATIN RIBBON:

3mm   Yellow 78in (2m)
1.5mm   Cornflower blue 78in (2m)

- Beadesign beads, one packet of gold 72
- Small piece of Vilene extra heavy interfacing, ⅜in (1cm) larger all round than the aperture of your card
- Card with an aperture of approximately 4½ x 2¾in (11.5 x 7cm)

Equipment

- Embroidery frame, 8 x 6in (20 x 15cm) or 6in (15cm) circular
- No. 24 tapestry needle for the cross stitch and the woven ribbon roses
- No. 7 embroidery needle
- Beading needle
- Embroidery scissors

PREPARATION

Stretch the fabric tightly in the circular frame or attach it to the rectangular frame with staples or drawing pins (see pages 14 and 16). If you use pins, cover the heads with masking tape to stop threads catching on them. Mark the centre of the fabric, both horizontally and vertically, with a light thread. Mark the size of the aperture of the card also with a light thread.

STITCHING

CROSS STITCH

See Stitching, page 115 for instructions on how to work the stitches, and refer to the Alphabet Charts on pages 122–124 for the letters. A chart from numbers 0 - 9 is given on page 125 for those who would like to celebrate a special birthday or anniversary in stitches.

Start from the centre of your fabric and, following the chart, count to the nearest stitch. Work all the cross stitch outline of the letter in double gold metallic thread. Remember that the top stitch of each cross must always lie in the same direction. Each cross is worked over one square of the fabric.

RIBBON EMBROIDERY

See Working with Ribbon, page 11. Refer often to the photograph opposite for positioning the ribbon.

Woven ribbon roses: With yellow Coton à Broder, make the foundation wheels for the roses, placing them along the letter approximately 1in (2.5cm) apart. Use the tapestry needle for weaving the yellow ribbon, remembering to start off by weaving quite firmly and then slacken off towards the end of the weaving.

Ribbon French knot flowers: Work five French knots in a circle, stitching with the 1.5mm blue ribbon. Ribbon French knots are worked in exactly the same way as the thread ones (see Stitching, page 118). Add a gold bead in the centre of each flower.

EMBROIDERY

See Stitching, page 115 for instructions on how to work the stitches.

Daisies: Work the daisies in white perlé thread using bullion stitches. Fan them out, and add three gold beads for the flower centres.

French knots: Fill the remaining spaces with French knots, using both green Coton à Broder threads. Mass them together to get a really raised effect.

FINISHING AND MAKING UP

Press any areas of the background fabric that you can reach without going over the ribbon. See Presentation, page 121, for instructions on how to make up the card.

Anniversary Cracker

GATHERED FLOWERS WITH EMBROIDERY AND BEADING

*This beautiful cracker is actually a glamorous wrapping for a distinctive present –
and then becomes an exquisite room decoration when it has done its job.
Extravagantly lace edged, entirely made from silver ribbon, it hides a padded and
lined cavity to take a gift for someone really special. The floral bouquet of the centre
panel is charmingly embroidered with ribbons, beads and French knots and is
bordered by an attractive combination of pink, green and silver ribbons,
picking up the colours of the embroidery.*

Materials

- Lining fabric, 32 x 12in (82 x 31cm)
- Evenweave fabric 14-count, 11 x 5in (28 x 12.5cm)
- Wadding (batting), sufficient to cover the tube
- Pregathered lace, white, ½in (1.25cm) wide, 3yd (3m)
- Cotton fabric in white, 21 x 12in (54 x 31cm)
- Firm Iron-on Vilene, 9½ x 9in (24 x 23cm)

RIBBON DESIGN SILK RIBBON,
3MM WIDE:

Deep peach 43, 18in (46cm)
Mid peach 168, 18in (46cm)
Paler peach 167, 36in (92cm)
Palest peach 166, 18in (46cm)
Creamy peach 39, 1½yd (1.4m)
Deep green 32, 1yd (92cm)
Paler green 31, 1yd (92cm)

- Panda double satin ribbon, 5mm wide, Flamingo 32, 2yd (1.8m)
- Madeira metallic No. 12, silver, one reel
- Gütermann sewing thread for stitching the silver ribbon, pale grey 224
- Panda polyester lamé ribbon, 35mm wide, colour 2 silver, 6½yd (6m)
- Panda polyester lamé ribbon, 3mm wide, colour 2 silver, 1yd (92cm)

BEADESIGN BEADS, ONE PACKET EACH OF:

Coral 49,   Silver 210,   Tan 76

- Card tube with 3in (7.5cm) diameter. A Pringle crisp carton was used for the finished example, the length and circumference of which are both approximately 9½in (24cm).

Equipment

- Embroidery frame, 12in (30cm) square
- No. 7 embroidery needle
- Beading needle
- Curved needle for the ladder stitch
- Embroidery scissors
- Sewing machine
- Tracing paper
- Sharp pencil
- Double-sided sticky tape

PREPARING THE CRACKER BODY

If you use a Pringles crisp tube, cut off ¼in (6mm) from each end. The measurements for this type of tube are used throughout. If you use a tube of different dimensions, alter the measurements accordingly.

Cut a piece of wadding (batting) 9in (23cm) square and a piece of the lining fabric 12in (30cm) square. Tack (baste) the wadding (batting) into the centre of the lining and stitch around the outside. Fold in half and stitch along the edge of the wadding (batting) to make a tube.

Put double-sided sticky tape on the outside edges of the ends of the cardboard tube. Insert the padded lining into the tube (with the wadding (batting) side to the card) and bring the lining material out over the tube ends and seal on to the double-sided sticky tape. Set this aside.

PREPARATION FOR EMBROIDERY

Tack (baste) the evenweave fabric over a 12in (30cm) square of cotton fabric and cut away the cotton at the back of the evenweave. Stretch the cotton fabric tightly on to the frame and secure with either staples or drawing pins. If you use pins cover the heads with masking tape to stop threads catching on them.

Mark a rectangle 9 x 3½in (23 x 9cm) in the centre of the evenweave fabric by tacking (basting) to give the embroidery area. Trace the design from the template on page 63 and lay on top of the evenweave embroidery area. Using a sharp pencil, mark the positions of the gathered ribbon petals for the circular flowers and the tall flower spikes.

STITCHING

RIBBON EMBROIDERY

See Working with Ribbon, page 11. Follow the template carefully and refer often to the detail photograph on page 63 and the photograph of the finished piece on page 61 for positioning the ribbon.

Gathered ribbon flowers: These are made up of five gathered silk ribbon petals. Use deepest peach for the lower left-hand flower, paler peach for the lower right-hand one, and palest peach for the top one.

Tall flowers: Work single gathered ribbon petals, and add ribbon French knots for the buds. Make leaves from small straight stitches in pale green ribbon .

Foliage: Work the green spikes on each side of the bouquet in straight stitches of pale green ribbon. The green stems are worked in both green ribbons in long straight stitches.

BEADING

See Stitching, page 115, for beading instructions.

Gathered ribbon flowers: Fill each centre with silver and tan beads.

Pale green spikes: Add silver beads in lines of three or four beads to the tips of the spikes.

Small bead flowers: Make these from circles of pink beads with one silver bead in the middle.

Beaded ribbons: Add the ribbons (see the template for colour order and ribbon position), attaching each to the fabric with beads as you go. Start with the creamy peach ribbon and use the lines of holes in the fabric to help with positioning the ribbons. Place the silver and green ribbons parallel to the creamy peach ribbon and fold these at each peak and at each edge. Attach the peach and green ribbons with silver beads and the silver ribbon with coral beads, using a beading needle.

FINISHING AND MAKING UP

CREATING THE FABRIC FOR THE MAIN BODY

Cut a piece of lining fabric 11 x 20in (28 x 51cm) and mark the centre across the narrow measurement.

Remove the embroidery from the frame, trim to ¾in (2cm) outside the line of tacking stitches, lay centrally over the lining fabric and tack (baste) into position.

Place the first rows of lace on either side of the embroidery, laying the lace edge up to the tacking stitches. Concentrating on one side first, tack (baste) in place and then lay the wide silver ribbon over the gathered edge. Tack (baste) and machine right on the edge using the grey Gütermann thread. Repeat this procedure once, using a second length of lace and of wide silver ribbon, leaving the edge of the second silver ribbon loose. Lay a third piece of silver ribbon up to the loose edge and machine this to the fabric, whilst still leaving the second ribbon loose.

Pleat a length of silver ribbon by marking along its edge with pins every 1½in (4cm), fold the ribbon in alternate directions so that the pins meet (see figs. 1 and 2).

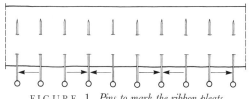

FIGURE 1 *Pins to mark the ribbon pleats*

Detail of central diamond panel

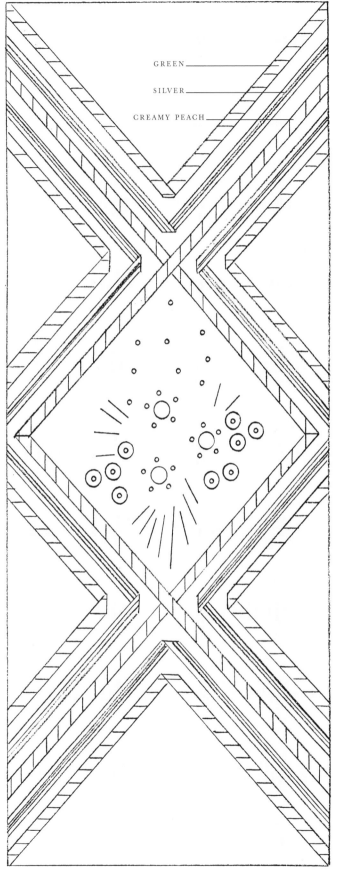

GREEN

SILVER

CREAMY PEACH

STITCH KEY

Round flower with five
gathered petals

Single gathered petal

Bead flower

Ribbon straight stitches

TEMPLATE *for Anniversary Cracker*

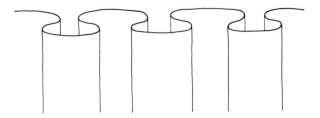

FIGURE 2 *Putting in the pleats*

Lay and tack the lace on to the pleated strip and then put the lace edge under the loose ribbon and over the stitched ribbon (see fig. 3). Work the second side to match.

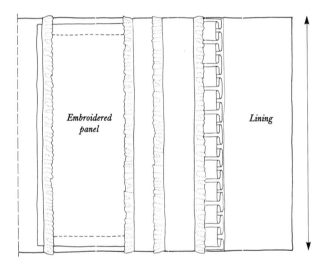

FIGURE 3 *Positioning the lace and the pleated strip*

MAKING THE CRACKER ENDS

Cut two pieces of white cotton fabric and two pieces of firm Iron-on Vilene, each 9½ x 4½in (24 x 11.5cm). Iron one piece of firm Vilene on to each piece of white cotton fabric.

**Working on to the Vilene side, add more ribbon and lace as shown in fig. 4, letting the ribbon and lace protrude 1in (2.5cm) over the edge at each side. The last piece of ribbon will protrude for half of its width over the end of the fabric.

Lay this piece under the cracker lining, right side to the reverse of the lining. Tack (baste) and stitch along the two side edges of the fabric and Vilene as this is cut

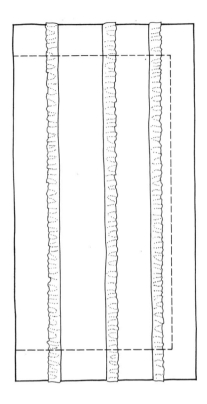

FIGURE 4 *Adding ribbon and lace*

to the finished size. Trim the seam and turn to the right side. Finger press the seams and lap the extending piece of ribbon back to the original lining and stitch. The piece of plain ribbon below the frill can then be lapped over the most recently added piece and stitched.

Make a channel for the ribbon ties by stitching across the full width of the fabric 3½in and 4in (9 cm and 10cm) from the end. Cut the 5mm peach ribbon in half and thread it through the channel.

Repeat the procedure from ** at the opposite end of the cracker fabric.

Wrap the completed cracker fabric around the prepared tube, positioning it carefully, and neatly ladder stitch the complete length of the cracker.

At the back of the cracker, pull up the peach ribbon to close one end and tie a bow as close as possible to the fabric. Bring the two free ends to the front of the cracker and tie a second bow.

Insert the gift into the cracker and tie the second ribbon in the same way.

Colours of Spring

Full of springtime brightness and hope, gathered flowers burst brilliantly out from a smooth background of cross stitch flowers and foliage. Framing the different elements of the design in couched ribbon gives an effective result that's easy to achieve. Traditional counted cross stitch – precise and measured – is a perfect foil for the freer style of contemporary ribbon embroidery.

Materials

- Evenweave fabric 22-count in cream, 12in (30cm) square

OFFRAY DOUBLE-FACE SATIN RIBBON, 3MM WIDE:

Light orchid (pale mauve) 430   2¼yd (2m)
Iris (deep mauve) 447   2¾yd (2.5m)
Yellow gold 660   20in (50cm)
Antique white SP 1961   20in (50cm)

MADEIRA SILK, ONE PACK EACH OF:

Dark green 1311   Cream 2014
Mid green 1408   Deep mauve 0713
Pale green 1309   Lavender 0902
Yellow 0113   Pale mauve 0801

- White perlé, one skein
- Flat wadding (batting) or Vilene extra heavy interfacing, 8in (20cm) square

Equipment

- Embroidery frame, 12in (30cm) square
- No. 24 tapestry needle for the cross stitch
- No. 7 embroidery needle for the ribbon work
- Embroidery scissors

PREPARATION

Stretch the fabric tightly on the embroidery frame. Secure with either staples or drawing pins (see page 14). If you use pins cover the heads with masking tape.

With a light coloured thread mark the vertical and horizontal centre lines of the fabric with a row of tacking (basting) stitches from top to bottom and side to side.

Mark out the position for the inner framework of the ribbon as follows: count 52 threads from the centre to the left, then 52 threads upwards; place a pin in this top left corner; repeat for the three remaining corners. The pins mark the inside points where the ribbons cross. The centre square should measure 104 threads in each direction. The ribbon width covers four threads.

Cut four lengths of 10in (25.5cm) of each of the two mauve ribbons. Couch each piece of ribbon into place with a single strand of a matching coloured silk. Work

the couching stitches every fourth thread of fabric (see Stitching, page 119). Start with the left-hand side inner ribbon – pale mauve – and work clockwise.

Next, place the four darker ribbons to make a square around the outside, leaving 24 threads between the two rows of ribbons. Couch.

STITCHING

CROSS STITCH

See Stitching, page 115 for instructions on how to work the stitches. Use a single strand of Madeira silk to work the cross stitches. Work each cross over two threads.

Start from the centre of the design. Complete all the cross stitches on the central design and borders before going on to the ribbon work.

RIBBON EMBROIDERY

See Working with Ribbon, page 11. Follow the chart carefully and refer often to the photograph on page 65 for colour and position of the ribbons.

Border flowers: Work three gathered ribbons in the spaces left between the cross stitches at either end of the side border designs and in the centre of the top and lower borders.

Large mauve flowers: Next work a circle of five ribbons in deep mauve for the centre of each of the three larger flowers. Then work a further circle of nine or ten ribbons around the outside in pale mauve.

Tall yellow and cream flowers: Work single gathered ribbon petals along the line of crosses that represent the stems.

EMBROIDERY

See Stitching, page 115, for instructions on how to work the stitches.

French knots: Using four strands of yellow Madeira silk, work a French knot in the centre of the large border cross stitch flowers. Using four strands of deep mauve Madeira silk, fill the centres of the large mauve flowers with French knots. Using four strands of Madeira silk in colours to match the ribbon, work French knots around the tall yellow and cream flowers. Start with four above the top ribbon, then work in the spaces.

Daisies: Using white perlé thread, work the daisies with fans of straight stitches radiating out from a yellow French knot.

Foliage: Add small straight stitches in pale green around the tall yellow and cream flowers.

FINISHING AND MAKING UP

See Presentation, page 120, for stretching, mounting and framing the picture.

STITCH KEY		
■ Madeira 0801	○ Madeira 1408	
▲ Madeira 0713	⁄⁄ Madeira 1309	
△ Madeira 0902	▽ Madeira 0113	
▶ Madeira 1311		

Dressing Table Set

WOVEN FLOWERS WITH RIBBON
EMBROIDERY, BLACKWORK AND BEADING

The elegant pattern for the background of this luxurious brush and mirror set was taken from an antique blackwork sampler. Worked in silver, with the addition of beadwork, it forms a filigree framework for the ribbon flowers. The backgound of the box lid also uses a filigree blackwork, but this time the posy of flowers is more naturalistic.

Brush and Mirror

Materials

- Brush and mirror set as supplied by Framecraft
- Aida Plus 14-count in ivory, 9 x 12in (23 x 30cm)

    OFFRAY EMBROIDERY RIBBON,
    ONE CARD EACH OF:
    4mm   Rosewood (maroon) 169
               Buttermilk 824
    2mm   Carnation 095
- Anchor Coton à Broder, deep pink, 970
- Madeira metallic No. 12, silver, two reels
- Beadesign beads, one packet of clover pink 8
- Sewing thread to match the beads

Equipment

- Rectangular embroidery frame (optional as this fabric is fairly stiff and can be worked in your hand)
- No. 24 tapestry needle for the woven ribbon roses and blackwork
- No. 7 embroidery needle
- Beading needle
- Tracing paper
- Sharp pencil

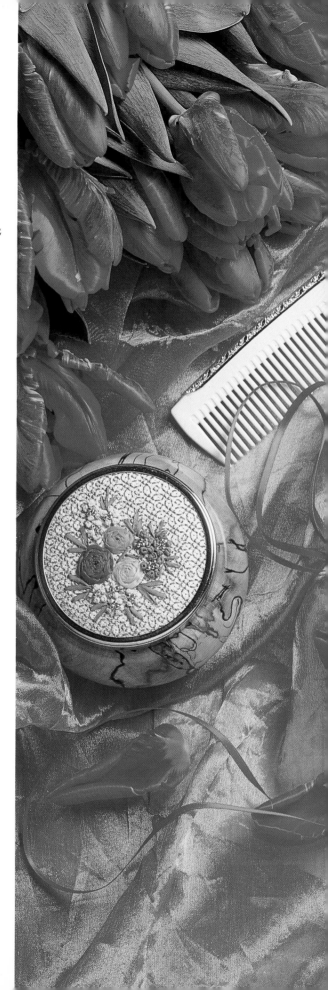

PREPARATION

If you use an embroidery frame, stretch the fabric tightly on the frame and secure with either staples or drawing pins (see page 14). If you use pins cover the heads with masking tape to stop threads catching on them. Trace the shape of the finished size required for the mirror back and the brush back and mark a vertical central line. Cut out the shapes and lay on the fabric, making sure that the central line is on the straight grain of the fabric. Tack (baste) around the edge, as close as possible to the outline, to use as a guide for the final cutting.

CHART *for Mirror Back*

STITCHING

THE MIRROR BACK
BLACKWORK

See Stitching, page 118, for instructions on how to work back stitch. Each square of the design represents one square of the fabric. Work with the sliver thread doubled. See Materials, page 10, for instructions on working with metallic threads.

Knot squares: Start at the top of the design with the first interlocking knot square, which is worked in back stitch. Work all three knot shapes, leaving a gap of four fabric squares between each one.

Background: Start by working outwards from the top

STITCH KEY

⊕ *Woven ribbon rose*

• *Silver bead*

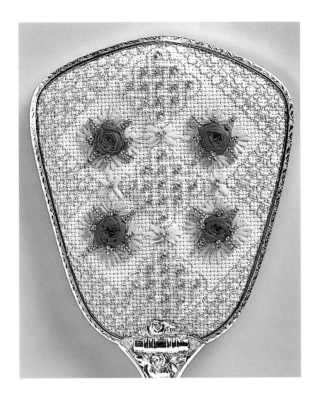

Detail of stitching and ribbon embroidery

knot shape as far as the tacking (basting) thread. Some of the shapes will be incomplete at the outside edge. Bear in mind that the tacking (basting) thread is the cutting guide and ensure that none of the metallic thread crosses over the tacking (basting).

RIBBON EMBROIDERY

See Working with Ribbon, page 11. Follow the chart on page 70 carefully and refer often to the detail photograph left for positioning the ribbon.

Woven ribbon roses: With the pink Coton à Broder, make four foundation wheels, each with seven spokes, placing them as shown on the design sheet. Use the tapestry needle for weaving the maroon ribbon, remembering to start off by weaving quite firmly and then slacken off towards the end of the weaving.

Pink daisies: Using the carnation ribbon, work each daisy as a fan of seven straight stitches, one on each side

(north, south, east and west) of each woven rose, with their centres towards the roses.

Cream daisies: Using the cream ribbon, work fans of straight stitches between each flower group.

BEADING

See Stitching, page 115. With a double sewing thread in the beading needle, place one bead at each intersection of the interlocking knot designs. Add three beads for each daisy flower centre and position spikes of four beads in between the daisy flowers.

CHART *for Brush Back*

STITCH KEY	
⊕	*Woven ribbon rose*
•	*Silver bead*

THE BRUSH BACK

Work similarly to the mirror back, starting with the central interlocking knot design and following chart for the inner boundary of the background stitching. Note that the lower woven rose has daisies only on its north, east and west sides.

FINISHING AND MAKING UP

Carefully cut around the tacked outline and set the work into the mirror and brush back, following the instructions given by the manufacturer.

Bowl Lid

These delightful little wooden bowls are made with the embroiderer in mind. We used Zweigart Aida 14-count in ivory for the lid, a specially processed fabric that can be cut without fraying. It can also be worked in your hand instead of in a frame.

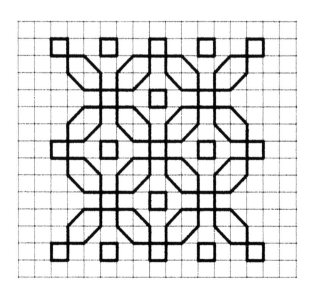

CHART *of Bowl Lid*

PREPARATION

Remove the small cardboard shape from the lid, lay this on the fabric and tack (baste) round it to outline the area

Materials

- Wooden bowl as supplied by Kernow Craft Woodturning
- Aida Plus 14-count in ivory, 4in (10cm) square
- Madeira metallic No.12, gold 33, one reel

OFFRAY EMBROIDERY RIBBON,
ONE CARD EACH OF:

4mm	Rosewood (deep pink) 169
	Tea rose (mid pink) 140
	Carnation (pale pink) 095
	Grape (mauve) 463
2mm	Baby maize (pale yellow) 617
	Moss (green) 570

- Beadesign beads, one packet of gold 72
- Anchor Coton à Broder deep pink 970

Equipment

- No. 24 tapestry needle for the woven ribbon roses
- No. 7 embroidery needle
- Beading needle
- Embroidery scissors

to be embroidered. Mark the centres of the three woven roses with a small dot, as shown in the template.

STITCHING

RIBBON EMBROIDERY

See Working with Ribbon, page 11. Follow the template opposite carefully and refer often to the detail photograph for positioning the ribbon.

Woven ribbon roses: Make three foundation wheels, each with seven spokes, placing them as shown on the template. Note that one of them is larger than the other two. Use the tapestry needle for weaving the ribbon, remembering to start off weaving quite firmly and then slacken off towards the end of the weaving. Work each rose in a different pink, with the largest in the deepest pink.

BLACKWORK

See Stitching, page 115, for instructions on how to work back stitch. Follow the chart shown opposite. Each square of the design represents one square of the fabric. Work with the gold thread doubled. See Materials, page 10, for instructions on working with metallic threads. Work the gold background up close to the woven roses and in between where possible.

RIBBON EMBROIDERY

Ribbon French knot flowers: There are three yellow French knot flowers on one side of the largest woven rose and four on the other. For each flower, work five French knots in a ring in pale yellow ribbon. Work the three mauve ribbon French knot flowers next; as the mauve ribbon is wider than the yellow, these will be slightly larger. Ribbon French knots are worked as thread ones (see Stitching, page 118).

Foliage: Work groups of straight stitches in green ribbon for the foliage, placing these where you feel they are needed.

BEADING

See Stitching, page 115. Using the beading needle, add three small gold beads to the centre of each yellow ribbon French knot flower, and five beads to the centre of each mauve ribbon French knot flower.

FINISHING AND MAKING UP

Once the stitching has been completed, cut out the circle of fabric close to the tacking (basting) stitches, removing any tacking (basting) threads that are left, taking care not to cut any of the gold threads.

Assemble the lid according to the instructions enclosed with the wooden bowl.

STITCH KEY	
⊛	*Woven ribbon rose*
°○°	*Round flower with five gathered petals*

TEMPLATE *for Bowl Lid*

Detail of stitching and ribbon embroidery

Wedding Garland Card

GATHERED RIBBON AND STITCHED RIBBON
FLOWERS WITH EMBROIDERY

A glorious memento of a special day, this card will bring back treasured memories for years to come. Heart and doves in shimmering silver provide a romantic background for the vibrant flower garland. The dramatic purple and yellow gold ribbons build up a splendid richness of colour and texture, providing a contrast with the lettering and numbers. Initially a card, but later a framed wedding sampler, this is a gift that the bride and groom will always treasure.

Materials

- 14-count fabric in cream, 9¾in (25cm) square

ANCHOR STRANDED COTTON (FLOSS),
ONE SKEIN EACH OF:

Dark green 258	Yellow 306
Light green 253	Mauve 109

OFFRAY EMBROIDERY RIBBON,
ONE CARD EACH OF:

2mm	Antique white 028
	Yellow gold 660
4mm	Grape 463
	Iris 447
7mm	Yellow gold 660

- Kreinik silver cord 001C, one reel
- Vilene extra heavy interfacing 7 x 5½in (18 x 14cm)
- Card with an aperture of 5½ x 4in (14 x 10cm)

PREPARATION

Stretch the fabric tightly in the circular frame or attach it to the rectangular frame with staples or drawing pins (see pages 14 and 16). If you use pins cover the heads with masking tape to stop threads catching on them. Mark the size of the aperture in the centre of the fabric using a light thread.

NOTE: The number of letters in a name vary so the design will alter slightly. If the bride's name is long, start the garland under the base of the letters (where the first purple gathered ribbon flower is on our card); if the groom's name is long, finish the garland above the top of the letters (where last purple gathered ribbon flower is on our card). If the names contain more than eight letters, leave only one square space between each letter.

STITCHING

CROSS STITCH

See Stitching, page 115, for instructions on how to work the stitches. The design is all worked in two strands of thread, except the French knots which are worked in six strands.

Names and date: Taking the correct letters from the

Equipment

- Embroidery frame, 8 x 6in (20 x 15cm) or 8in (20cm) circular
- Embroidery scissors
- No. 24 tapestry needle for the cross stitch
- No. 7 embroidery needle for the ribbon work

chart and leaving two square spaces between each letter, stitch the cross stitch name of the bride in mauve at the top of the work. The first letter starts three squares from both the top and the side on the left.

Next work the date, using the numbers from the chart and spacing them evenly across the work. The groom's name starts four square spaces above the date. To position it correctly, start with the final letter to the extreme right and work the name backwards.

Cross stitch: Work the metal thread cross stitch, starting with the top right hand bird at the top of his tail. With a short name this can be level with the lower edge of the letters, as in the finished example, but if a longer name is required, drop down two square spaces. Complete the bird and continue with the heart and the lower bird. Add a French knot eye to each bird.

When you have finished the heart and birds, work the line of green cross stitch which is a position guide for the ribbon embroidered garland.

RIBBON EMBROIDERY

See Working with Ribbon, page 11. Follow the design carefully and refer often to the photograph opposite for colour and positioning the ribbon.

The garland is made up of a number of different flowers scattered along the line of green cross stitches. Don't try to copy our example exactly; work each type of flower separately, spacing them along the garland. Hold your work out at arms length every now and then, and you will soon see where another flower is needed.

Gathered ribbon flowers: Work three gathered ribbon petals in grape for each large purple flower. The small mauve flowers and the yellow gold flowers

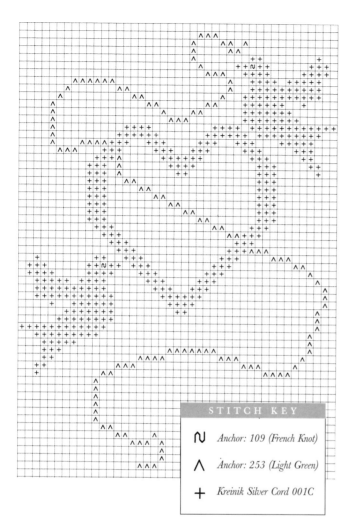

(worked with 7mm ribbon) are individual gathered ribbon petals.

Stitched ribbon white and yellow daisies: Work fans of straight stitches in 2mm ribbon.

EMBROIDERY

French knots: Fill the centres of the round grape flowers with yellow French knots. Give each daisy a yellow French knot centre. Work small groups of French knots in mauve and yellow in spaces around the flowers.

Foliage: When all the flowers are worked, add straight stitches in pale green and finally more straight stitches in dark green to add depth.

FINISHING AND MAKING UP

While the embroidery is still on the frame, attach the Vilene behind the work, positioning the design centrally. Stitch round the outside with small running stitches. This will help with stretching the work in the card. Press any areas of the background fabric that you can reach without going over the ribbon. See Presentation, page 121, for instructions on how to make up the card.

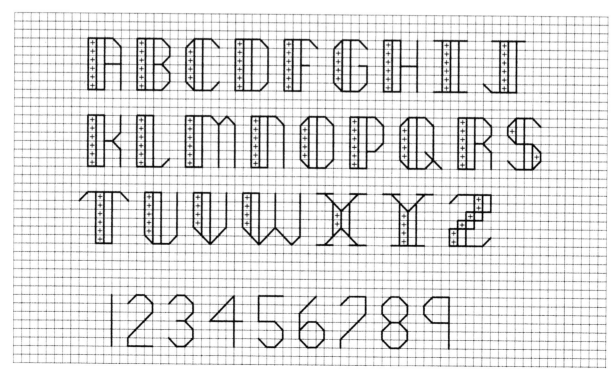

Framed by Flowers

GATHERED RIBBON FLOWERS, STITCHED RIBBON, EMBROIDERY AND BEADING

A favourite photograph will look even more special framed by this beautiful embroidered border. The background of closely-worked cushion stitches in a mix of variegated pink and mauve lends an almost marble-like quality to the frame, which is enhanced by the overlay of silver threads. In contrast, the flowers are worked in gentle, naturalistic swathes. To spikes of cool cream gathered ribbon flowers are added stitched gold ribbon flowers and white daisies, all given centres of gold beads and surrounded by foliage. The result is magical.

Materials

- Congress cloth (sometimes called coin net),10 x 12in (25.5 x 30cm)
- Lining material in white, 10 x 12in (25.5 x 30cm)
- Indian rayon thread, one spool each of: Variegated pink and pale mauve
- Madeira metallic No. 12, silver, one reel

OFFRAY EMBROIDERY RIBBON,
ONE CARD EACH OF:

4mm	Ivory 810
	Buttermilk 824
	Yellow gold 660
2mm	Yellow gold 660
	Antique white 028
	Acid green 556
	Grass green 584

- Beadesign beads, one packet each of: Gold 72; Bronze 69
- Vilene extra heavy interfacing, 10 x 8in (25.5 x 20cm)
- Panda metallic piping, 2¼yd (2m)
- Panda polyester lamé ribbon, 35mm wide, silver, 39in (1m) (optional)

PREPARATION

Stretch the coin net on to the embroidery frame and secure with either staples or drawing pins (see page 14).

Equipment

- Embroidery frame, 10 x 12in (25.5 x 30cm)
- No. 24 tapestry needle for the canvas work
- No. 7 embroidery needle
- Beading needle
- Small curved needle
- Embroidery scissors
- Strutted picture frame back 10 x 8in (25.5 x 20cm)
- Mount card, two pieces, each 10 x 8in (25.5 x 20cm)
- Double-sided tape
- Needlework finisher and small paint brush

If you use pins cover the heads with masking tape to stop threads catching on them.

STITCHING

CANVAS WORK

See Stitching, page 115, for instructions on how to work the stitches.

Cushion stitch: Using two long threads of variegated pink plus one long thread of pale mauve together in the needle and doubled over (to give six threads to work with), begin the stitching. The squares of cushion stitch are worked over eight threads (see fig.1, page 78). It is easier to work the central stitch of the square (the

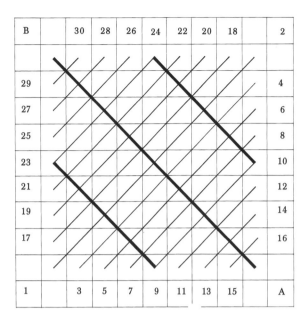

B		30	28	26	24	22	20	18		2
29										4
27										6
25										8
23										10
21										12
19										14
17										16
1		3	5	7	9	11	13	15		A

F I G U R E 1 *Showing the cushion stitching with*
the three overlaying stitches

longest) and then work either side of that stitch, going
over one fewer intersection of the canvas with each
stitch and completing the other side of the square in the
same way. The squares are worked with the stitches
lying in alternate directions (see the photograph on page
81 for detail). Fig. 2 on page 80 shows the number of
squares to be stitched.

Overlaying: Use the silver thread doubled. Thread
the needle and pull through a suitable length, cut the
ends to match. Run your finger down each thread in
turn and release, to allow any twist to come out, and
then knot the ends by wrapping the thread round your
finger and stitching into it twice.

Over each cushion stitch square work three
overlaying stitches as shown in fig. 1. Work the overlay
stitches in the opposite direction from the cushion
stitches.

Framed by Flowers
and Wedding Bag (see page 83)

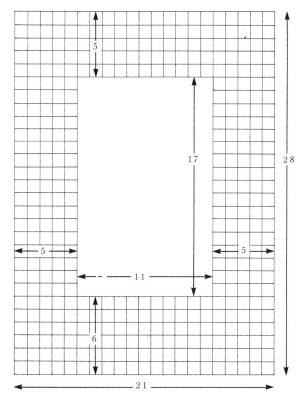

FIGURE 2 *Showing the number of squares of cushion stitch*

RIBBON EMBROIDERY

See Working with Ribbon, page 15. Refer often to template on page 82 and the photograph on page 81 for positioning the ribbon.

Tall flowers, lower right hand corner: Begin at their tops with the single gathered ribbon flowers. Work each of the medium sized flowers as groups of three single gathered ribbon petals. The largest flowers each have five gathered ribbon petals.

Oval yellow gold flowers: Use the tapestry needle to work 4mm wide yellow gold ribbon as straight stitches through the canvas. The straight stitches all point to the centre of the flower. Remember to leave a small area for attaching the bead centres.

White daisies: Work as fans of straight stitches in white ribbon.

Foliage: Using the two green 2mm ribbons, work fans of straight stitches to represent the foliage and small straight stitches surrounding the flowers.

French knots: Place green ribbon French knots between the lower flowers. Ribbon French knots are worked in exactly the same way as the thread ones (see Stitching, page 118).

Flowers, upper left hand corner: These are worked similarly to the lower flowers.

BEADING

See Stitching, page 115. Using the beading needle, add all the bead centres – gold beads for all but the daisies, where the bronze ones are used.

FINISHING AND MAKING UP

Cut a piece of mounting card ⅛in (3mm) smaller in each dimension than the finished embroidery area. Cut the Vilene slightly smaller than the card and use either double-sided tape or glue to fix it to the card.

Cut away the canvas to within ¾in (2cm) of the stitches around the outside and in the aperture. Using a small paint brush, apply needlework finisher to all the corners, both in the aperture and on the outside. Allow to dry thoroughly before cutting diagonally into the aperture corners, taking care not to cut the stitching.

Lay the embroidery face down and place the Vilene over the back. Apply double-sided tape to the back of the card mount and position this, tape uppermost, on the Vilene and pull the canvas edges tightly over the card on to the double-sided tape. Cut away some of the excess canvas at the outside corners. Lace the back of the canvas to hold it in place.

Attach the silver piping to the edges, working from the right side and stitching carefully to ensure that the stitches do not show.

Cut the second piece of card to fit over the back and cover it with white lining fabric. Position the photograph and attach this to the card back. Using a curved needle, sew the embroidered front and backing card together. Stick the strutted back to the backing card. For extra neatness, stitch the wide silver ribbon behind the piping and stick over the edges of the strutted back.

FRAMED BY FLOWERS
Detail of ribbon embroidery

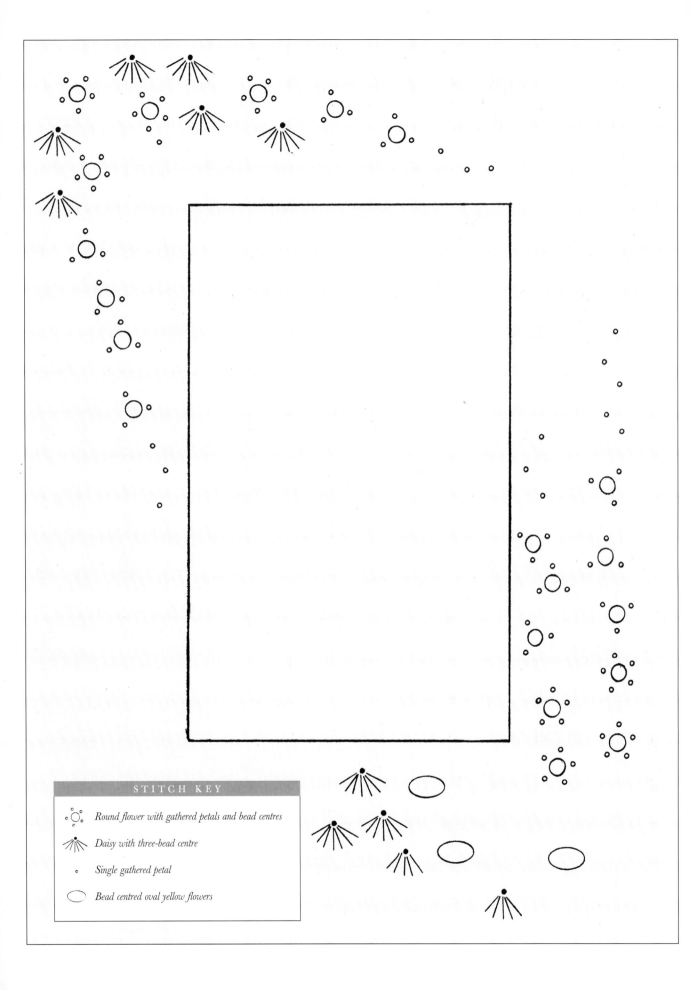

STITCH KEY

Round flower with gathered petals and bead centres

Daisy with three-bead centre

Single gathered petal

Bead centred oval yellow flowers

Wedding Bag

WOVEN AND GATHERED RIBBON FLOWERS
WITH EMBROIDERY AND BEADING

*Silver lamé ribbon and metallic piping are joined to make the luxurious fabric of
this elegant wedding bag. Continuing this extravagant theme, the flap is adorned
with woven ribbon roses, gathered ribbons, beads and French knots massed together
to give a rich border. An exclusive and stylish design, this could be a beautiful
accessory for a bride, or even her bridesmaid or mother.*

Materials

- Cotton fabric, 10in (25.5cm) square
- Evenweave fabric in white or cream, 12 x 4in
  (30 x 10cm)
- Lining fabric in pink, 18 x 11in (46 x 28cm)

ANCHOR COTON À BRODER,
ONE SKEIN EACH OF :

White 1	Pink 26
Cream 275	

OFFRAY EMBROIDERY RIBBON, 4MM WIDE,
ONE CARD EACH OF:

Ultra violet 467	Carnation 095
Sweet nectar 161	Ivory 810

- Gütermann sewing thread in pale grey, one reel
- Madeira metallic No. 12, silver, one reel

BEADESIGN BEADS, ONE PACKET EACH OF:

Mauve 19	Pink 4
Silver 110	Green 32

- Panda polyester lamé ribbon in silver, 35mm wide,
  5½yd (5m)
- Panda piping in silver, 3¼yd (3m)
- Vilene extra heavy interfacing 16½ x 9in (42 x 23cm)
- One silver press stud

PREPARATION

Put the cotton fabric into the circular frame and tack
(baste) the rectangle of evenweave fabric over it. Trace
the template on page 84 and cut out; place it centrally

Equipment

- Embroidery frame 10in (25.5 cm) circular
- Embroidery scissors
- No. 24 tapestry needle for the woven ribbon roses
- No. 7 embroidery needle
- Tracing paper
- Sharp pencil
- Sewing machine

over the evenweave fabric and tack round it to mark its
position. On the tracing paper, cut out the circles which
position the woven roses and, with a large needle pierce
each small circle - these show the position of the
gathered ribbons. Lay the tracing paper back on to the
fabric inside the tacked outline and, with a sharp pencil,
make a dot for each gathered ribbon and stencil the
positions of the circles for the woven roses.

RIBBON EMBROIDERY

See Working with Ribbon, page 11. Refer often to the
photograph on pages 78–79 for positioning the ribbon.
Woven ribbon roses: With pink Coton à Broder,
make ten foundation wheels, each with seven spokes,
placing them as shown on the template. Use the tapestry
needle for weaving the ribbon, remembering to start off
by weaving quite firmly and then slacken off towards the

end of the weaving. Refer to the photograph for positioning of the colours.

Gathered ribbon flowers: Work the pink and ivory flowers as single gathered ribbon petals.

EMBROIDERY

See Stitching, page 115, for instructions on how to work the stitches. For the remainder of the design, you are filling in the background so you need not refer to the chart.

French knots: Using cream Coton à Broder, work groups of three French knots, spacing them throughout the embroidered area. Follow these with groups of pink, white and silver French knots.

BEADING

See Stitching, page 115. Using the beading needle and matching thread, stitch on the beads in groups of three, starting with the mauve beads, followed by silver, pink and finally the turquoise beads.

The embroidered area should be almost filled. Check for any gaps and fill with silver French knots.

FINISHING AND MAKING UP

Cut out the Vilene according to the bag pattern, fig. 1. Lay the embroidered panel tracing (this includes the allowed turnings) over the flap end and mark its position with the sharp pencil.

The bag fabric is made from the wide lamé ribbon and the silver piping. The finished fabric should be large enough to cover the Vilene with at least ½in (1.25cm) extra each side. Notice that the lower sloped edge needs only to extend ½in (1.25cm) below the marked line.

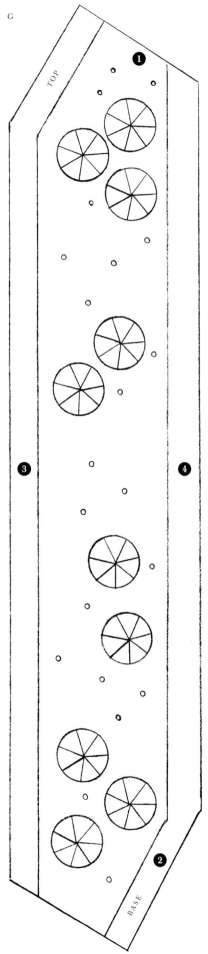

STITCH KEY		
 Woven ribbon rose	◦	Single gathered ribbon petal

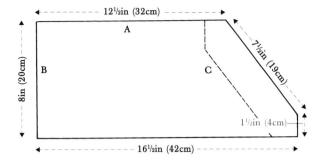

FIGURE 1 *Bag Pattern*

Cut a piece of wide lamé ribbon 11½in (29cm) long, and lay this on the Vilene so that ½in (1.25cm) protrudes over the edge marked A in fig. 1. Cut a similar length of piping cord and lay this over the edge of the ribbon so that half the width of the white area of piping cord is on the ribbon and half protruding over the edge (see fig. 2).

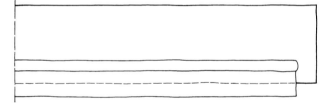

FIGURE 2 *First layer of ribbon with piping cord laid along its edge*

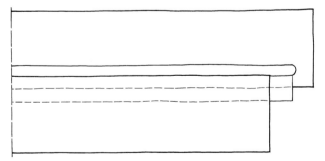

FIGURE 3 *Second piece of ribbon in position*

Cut a second piece of ribbon ½in (1.25cm) longer than the first (this is to ensure that the marked line on the Vilene is covered) and lay this so that its edge is right up to the silver part of the piping cord (see fig. 3). Stitch as close to the piping cord as you can, either by hand or by machine. Keep working in this way, extending the lower edge to cover your pencil mark, until all the Vilene is covered and there is sufficient ribbon to turn over the far edge. Fold the extra ribbon over the edge on the sides of the Vilene and hem down.

Using a length of the silver ribbon as a binding, bind the end marked B in fig. 1 by laying the ribbon over the right side and machine and then turning the ribbon over to the wrong side and hemming in place. Neaten the ends as you proceed.

Return to the embroidered area and, still using the silver ribbon, tack (baste) lengths to each side in order 1–4, as indicated on the template. The remaining two sides are turned in without a binding. It is easier to stitch this by hand so that you can get really close to the embroidered edges.

Remove the fabric from the frame and trim away the excess fabric below the ribbon binding. Finger press the bindings away from the embroidery and start to pin in place over the flap end of the prepared bag fabric, turning under the top edge marked C in fig. 1, and laying the ribbon over the Vilene at the sides and lower edge. Tack (baste) and stitch into place.

Cut the lining fabric to the bag template adding ½in (1.25cm) turnings and, folding the edges under, pin, tack (baste) and finally hem into position close to the edge but so that it does not show on the outside.

Fold the fabric into three, forming the bag shape, creasing well along the folds. Ladder stitch the sides together with the grey thread. Do this carefully so that the stitches do not show. A neat inside finish can be obtained by stitching tiny beads all along the edges of the lining on the flap.

Stitch one half of the press stud at the extreme point of the lower edge of the flap and then the other half to the bottom edge of the bag.

Prayer Book Cover

WOVEN AND GATHERED RIBBON FLOWERS, EMBROIDERY AND BEADING

What bride would not be proud to carry her prayer book in this cover on her wedding day? The careful gradation of colour surrounding the central cross with a special aura is cleverly reversed for the stitched background and the design is repeated on the front and back of the cover. The fabric is constructed from silver lamé ribbon.

The measurements in the materials list and in the text are for a cover made for The Sunday Service Book printed by the Oxford University Press.

Materials

- Congress cloth (sometimes called coin net), 12 x 14in (30 x 35.5cm)

INDIAN RAYON THREAD, ONE SPOOL EACH OF:

White	Deep pink
Cream	Pale turquoise
Deep cream	Deep turquoise
Pale pink	

OFFRAY EMBROIDERY RIBBON, ONE CARD EACH OF:

4mm	Colonial rose 168
	Moonstone 203
	Buttermilk 824
	Tropic 323
7mm	Colonial rose 168

- Sewing thread, one reel of silver grey
- Madeira metallic No. 12, silver, three reels
- Beadesign beads, one packet each of: silver 210; turquoise 21
- Vilene extra heavy interfacing cut to the dimensions of the outer cover of the book
- Panda polyester lamé ribbon in silver, 3mm wide, 2¼yd (2m)
- Panda polyester lamé ribbon in silver, 35mm wide, 3¼yd (3m)
- DMC Coton à Broder, pink 603

Equipment

- Embroidery frame, 12 x 14in (30 x 35.5cm)
- No. 24 tapestry needle for the canvas work
- No. 7 embroidery needle
- Beading needle
- Embroidery scissors

PREPARATION

To arrive at the correct dimensions for your book fold a piece of paper around it, turning the edges in like a book jacket. Mark the paper where the front cover starts and another where the back cover finishes and also mark the depth of the book at the top and bottom edges. Lay the paper flat and join these marks to give the outline of the book. Add an ⅛in (3mm) frame all round to give the finished size of the cover. Add a further 1½in (4cm) minimum all round to give the size of coin net and embroidery frame you need.

Stretch the coin net on to the embroidery frame and secure with either staples or drawing pins (see page 14). If you use pins cover the heads with masking tape to stop threads catching on them.

Mark the congress cloth with the following dimensions: a) the finished size of your Prayer Book cover; b) the border for the ribbon binding; c) the position of the spine of the book. Fig. 1 shows the markings used for our Prayer Book cover.

Detail of Prayer Book Cover, front and spine

Mark the centre of the top of the front of the cover for positioning the cross. Cut two pieces of paper each ⅝in (1.5cm) wide and, placing one of these vertically, use the second horizontally to determine the final position of the bar of the cross. See fig. 1 for the position of the cross in our worked example.

STITCHING

NOTE: All the stitching details given are for our worked example; adjustments will need to be made for a smaller or larger book.

EMBROIDERY AND BEADING

See Stitching (page 115) for instructions on how to work the stitches. When using the Indian rayon thread you will need three long lengths in the needle which are then doubled over to give six thicknesses.

Rhodes stitch cross: Start working downwards from the top of the cross on the front cover, using the central eight threads for the Rhodes stitches. The top Rhodes stitch is in white Indian rayon thread, the second in cream, then deep cream, pale pink and deep pink. Leave four threads unused (for the top horizontal ribbon) and then work one Rhodes stitch in white for the centre of the cross. Leave a gap of four threads (for the bottom horizontal ribbon) and then work downwards in Rhodes stitches using the following

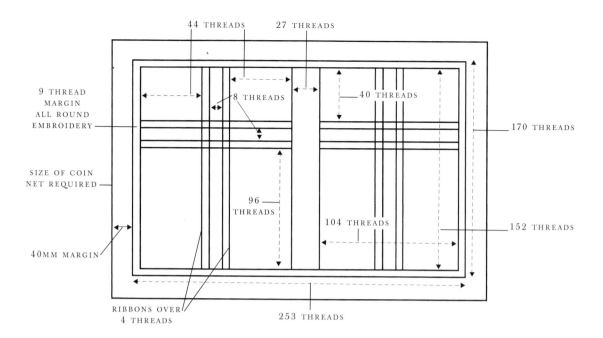

44 THREADS   27 THREADS

9 THREAD
MARGIN
ALL ROUND
EMBROIDERY

8 THREADS

40 THREADS

170 THREADS

SIZE OF COIN
NET REQUIRED

96
THREADS

104 THREADS

152 THREADS

40MM MARGIN

RIBBONS OVER
4 THREADS

253 THREADS

FIGURE 1 *Plan for Prayer Book stitching*

combinations of Indian rayon threads in your needle:

1ST STITCH: Three deep pink threads.

2ND STITCH: Two deep pink and one pale pink threads.

3RD STITCH: One deep pink and two pale pink threads.

4TH STITCH: Three pale pink threads.

5TH STITCH: Two pale pink and one deep cream thread.

6TH STITCH: One pale pink and two deep cream threads.

7TH STITCH: Three deep cream threads.

8TH STITCH: Two deep cream and one cream thread.

9TH STITCH: One deep cream and two cream threads.

10TH STITCH: Three cream threads.

11TH STITCH: Two cream and one white thread.

12TH STITCH: Three white threads.

For the horizontal bar of the cross, work outwards, leaving four threads on each side of the central white Rhodes stitch for the ribbon. Start with deep pink, then pale pink, deep cream, cream and finally white.

Place lengths of 3mm silver ribbon on either side of the rows of Rhodes stitches and attach with the tiny turquoise beads, placing each one in line with the edges of the Rhodes stitches, using the beading needle (see Stitching, page 115).

RIBBON EMBROIDERY

See Working with Ribbon, page 11. Refer often to the photograph on page 87 for positioning the ribbon.

Woven ribbon roses: With Coton à Broder, make eight foundation wheels, each with seven spokes, placing them as shown on the template. Use the tapestry needle for weaving the ribbon, remembering to start off by weaving quite firmly and then slacken off towards the end of the weaving.

Single gathered ribbon flowers: Using the 7mm colonial rose, and the 4mm buttermilk ribbons, scatter these amongst the roses, working a French knot in the centre of each, using six thickness of deep cream thread.

Floral background: Fill in the background space with cream rayon thread French knots, turquoise (Tropic) ribbon French knots (worked in exactly the same way as the thread ones), turquoise and silver beads and finally completely fill the remaining spaces with deep pink French knots, again using the rayon thread.

BACKGROUND EMBROIDERY AND BEADING

See Stitching, page 115 for information on how to work the stitches.

Rice stitch: Work each large cross over four threads of the coin net. Start above the horizontal bar of the cross, following the shape of the floral area and working outwards diagonally. In the example, one row of each colour of the Indian rayon threads has been worked in the order shown in the materials list, arriving at the deep turquoise in the top corners.

Beneath the horizontal bar of the cross the stitches again are worked in rows that follow the shape of the floral area. Our illustrated cover starts with a single row of each of the white, cream and deep cream and then two rows each of the other colours, finishing in the corners with deep turquoise. Concentrate on getting the effect of the colour graduating from white, through the creams and pinks, to turquoise; but, so long as you start with the white and finish with deep turquoise, the proportions in between are not really important.

Complete each rice stitch by crossing the corners using metallic silver thread.

The spine: Work two vertical rows of Rhodes stitch over eight threads, with a gap of eight threads between the rows for the ribbon and beads. Starting from the top, the Rhodes stitches are worked in the following order: 1st stitch – white; 2nd stitch – cream; 3rd stitch – deep cream; 4th stitch – pale pink; 5th stitch – deep pink; 6th stitch – pale pink; 7th stitch – deep cream; 8th stitch – cream; 9th stitch – white; 10th stitch – deep pink; 11th stitch – white; 12th stitch – cream; 13th stitch – deep cream; 14th stitch – pale pink; 15th stitch – deep pink; 16th stitch – pale pink; 17th stitch – deep cream; 18th stitch – cream; 19th stitch – white.

Lay two pieces of 3mm silver ribbon along the centre of the spine and couch over one, under the other and back over the second one – forming a 'figure of eight' in stitching – do this over every eighth thread. Stitch on the beads in groups vertically as follows: turquoise – silver – silver – turquoise, in line with each of the Rhodes stitches so that the beads lie between the two rows of ribbon.

Back cover: Work the cross in Rhodes stitch and ribbon as for the front cover. Work the background in horizontal rows of rice stitch, starting with deep pink at the top and bottom edges, graduating the colours in the reverse order to those used for the vertical of the cross,

working two rows of rice stitch, each over four threads, to each rhodes stitch.

FINISHING AND MAKING UP

Remove the coin net from the frame and cut out the shape marked for the finished cover. Bind the top and lower edges with 35mm silver ribbon: lay the ribbon right side to the canvas and attach right against the edges of the canvas work stitches with back stitch, or by using a sewing machine. Cut two further pieces of ribbon of the same length and stitch these to the binding ribbon to give a double width. Fold the ribbon on the line of the stitching before binding the two side edges in the same way.

Cut the Vilene to the size of the embroidered area and position on the reverse side. Along the long edges, pull the ribbon over the Vilene and attach with herring-bone stitch (see Stitching, page 115). Fold over the ribbons attached to the short edges in the same way and stitch to the Vilene with herring bone stitch.

Cut four lengths of 35mm ribbon each approximately 4in (10cm) longer than the finished cover and stitch them together lengthways in pairs. Fold the ends under to exactly match the cover and attach across top, side and bottom to form flaps to enable the book covers to fit inside (fig. 1).

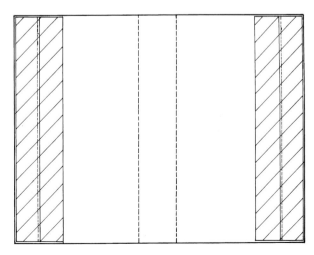

FIGURE 1 *Making the flaps*

Wedding Ring Cushion

WOVEN AND GATHERED FLOWERS,
EMBROIDERY AND BEADING

Delicate froths of white organdie surround this fairy-tale cushion, framing a silken delight sparkling with the richness of silver and gold. Garlands of cascading flowers in white, antique white and pearl, create beautiful settings for the rings carefully tied to the cushion in fine satin ribbon.

It's a stunning combination that creates a romantic centrepiece for a church or register office wedding, or for a blessing ceremony where rings are exchanged.

Finely worked in exquisite detail, this Wedding Cushion will become an heirloom, a lasting memento of that special day for you to treasure in years to come.

Equipment

- Embroidery frame, 18 x 14in (46 x 35.5cm)
- No. 24 tapestry needle for the woven ribbon roses
- No. 7 embroidery needle
- Beading needle
- Embroidery scissors
- Tracing paper
- Sharp pencil

Wedding Ring Cushion and Prayer Book Cover (see page 86)

Materials

- Closely-woven cushion fabric in white, two pieces, each 18 x 14in (46cm x 35.5cm)
- Offray double face satin ribbon, 3mm wide, white, 2¼yd (2m)
- Offray Embroidery Ribbon 4mm wide, antique white 028, one card
- Kreinik metallics Balger ribbon, 1/16in (1.5mm) wide, pearl 032, one card
- Anchor Coton à Broder, white, one skein
- Madeira metallic No 12, silver, one reel
- Beadesign beads, one packet each of: silver 210; green 037
- Panda Polyester organdie Wedding-Print ribbon, 35mm wide, Silver/white 4636, 1¾yd (1.5m)
- Panda organdie ribbon, 50mm wide, white 4628, 3¼yd (3m)
- Panda organdie ribbon, 20mm wide, white 4628, 3¼yd (3m)
- Foam cushion pad, 1¼in (3cm) thick, 9½ x 12in (24 x 31cm)
- Cotton fabric in white to cover pad

PREPARATION

Stretch the cushion fabric tightly on the embroidery frame. Secure with either staples or drawing pins (see page 14). If you use pins cover the heads with masking tape to stop threads catching on them.

Trace the template on page 93 and lay the tracing paper under the fabric. Mark the dots for the round flowers, woven roses and daisy centres. Lightly mark the positions for the ribbon bow and encircling garlands. If the fabric is too dense for you to see the traced design, place the tracing paper on top of the fabric and pierce the paper with a sharp pencil (see page 16).

STITCHING

RIBBON EMBROIDERY

See Working with Ribbon, page 11. Refer often to the photograph on page 94 for positioning the ribbon.

Gathered ribbon flowers: Using the double-sided satin ribbon, work five gathered ribbon petals for each round flower.

Woven ribbon roses: With white Coton à Broder, make eighteen foundation wheels, each with seven spokes, placing them as shown on the template. Use the tapestry needle for weaving the Offray Embroidery Ribbon, remembering to start off by weaving quite firmly and then slacken off towards the end of the weaving.

Daisies: Work fans of straight stitches in Kreinik ribbon for the petals.

BEADING

For instructions on beading see Stitching, page 115. Using the beading needle, add spikes of four silver beads around the flowers where the spaces allow. Add the green beads in groups of three.

Gathered ribbon flowers: Add silver beads to the centres of the round flowers, leaving some spaces for French knots.

EMBROIDERY

See Stitching, page 115, for instructions on how to work the stitches.

Ribbon garland: Outline the garland in silver metallic thread using back stitch. Finish by working chain stitches along the centre of the garlands using white Coton à Broder.

Gathered ribbon flowers: Fill the round flower centres with Coton à Broder French knots between the silver beads.

Daisies: Work three French knots for the centre of each flower.

RIBBON BORDER AND RING TIES

The outer measurements of the cushion are 9 x 11½in (23 x 29cm). Mark these dimensions on your fabric with tacking (basting) stitches, making sure the embroidery design is in the centre of the rectangle.

Organdie patterned ribbon: This ribbon is too

STITCH KEY

Round flowers

Daisy flowers

Woven roses

TEMPLATE *for Wedding Ring Cushion*

springy to make mitred corners satisfactorily, so lay two pieces along the side edges first, inside the tacking (basting) line, and then lay the top and lower ribbons so that they overlap the side ribbons at the corners. Tack (baste) these ribbons in position and then attach them to the cushion fabric with white Coton à Broder French knots along the inner and outer edges.

Ribbon ties for the two rings: Using double-sided white ribbon, cut two lengths, approximately 11in (28cm) each. Fold them in half and attach them, at the middle, just under the group of three roses at the top of the flower circle. Finish these by adding a silver bead.

FINISHING AND MAKING UP

Organdie ribbon edging: Tack (baste) the two 3¹/₄yd (3m) lengths of organdie ribbon together along one edge and then pleat them ready to surround the

Detail of ribbon embroidery

cushion. Tack (baste) the pleats into place, then put the ribbon and the right side of the embroidery together, edges matching. Tack (baste).

Lay the second piece of cushion fabric on top of the embroidered surface, right side to the embroidery, and tack (baste) together, sandwiching the frill between the two pieces of fabric. Tack (baste) and stitch together on three sides, then turn the cushion cover to the outside.

For the illustrated example, we used a piece of 1¹/₄in (3cm) thick foam for the pad. This was covered in white cotton fabric and made a good, firm cushion. Place the pad inside the cushion cover. Turn in the raw edges on the fourth side, sandwich the frill, and ladder stitch by hand (see Stitching, page 119).

Seasonal Greetings

STITCHED RIBBON, EMBROIDERY,
BEADING AND QUILTING

The dramatic combination of Christmas reds and greens make this the perfect card to send with your Seasonal Greetings. Surrounded by holly leaves and berries, fir cones and foliage and with a background of quilted silver lamé ribbon, the two magnificent poinsettias capture the mood of the festivities.

Materials

- Cotton fabric in white, 10in (25.5cm) square
- Evenweave fabric with a silver metallic thread, 5in (12.5cm) square
- Panda silver lamé ribbon, 35mm wide, two 6in (15cm) lengths

OFFRAY EMBROIDERY RIBBON,
4MM WIDE, ONE CARD EACH OF:

Blended bronze 846   Grass green 584
Poppy 235

ANCHOR STRANDED COTTON (FLOSS),
ONE SKEIN EACH OF :

Bright red 046   Mid green 255
Brown 355   Dark green 258
Pale green 264

BEADESIGN BEADS, ONE PACKET EACH OF:
Gold 72; Green 37; Red 56; Black 78

- Vilene extra heavy interfacing, 6in (15cm) square

Equipment

- Embroidery frame, 8in (20cm) circular
- No. 24 tapestry needle for the ribbon embroidery
- No. 7 embroidery needle
- Beading needle
- Embroidery scissors
- Green folded card with 4in (10cm) aperture

PREPARATION

Tack (baste) the square of evenweave fabric to the centre of the white cotton fabric. Position the two pieces of silver lamé ribbon on each side, leaving a gap of 1½in (4cm) between them, and tack (baste) down each side of the ribbon. Stretch the fabric tightly into the circular frame. Using the aperture of the card as a guide, tack (baste) the outline of a 4in (10cm) square in the centre of the fabric to ensure that the design is well-positioned.

STITCHING

RIBBON EMBROIDERY

See Working with Ribbon, page 11. Refer often to the photograph on page 95 for positioning the ribbon.

Poinsettias: Mark the centre of the top poinsettia 1in (2.5cm) from the top and ¾in (2cm) from the edge of the right-hand silver lamé ribbon. Mark the centre of the lower poinsettia 1½in (4cm) from the lower edge and ¾in (2cm) in from the left-hand silver lamé ribbon edge.

Thread the tapestry needle with the red ribbon and come up to the right-hand side just below the top flower centre mark. Lay the ribbon down to form an outer petal. Using two strands of red stranded cotton (floss) in the embroidery needle, bring the needle up at the petal's tip, encircle the ribbon and take the needle back down through the fabric immediately beside the original entry point: this will squeeze the ribbon and form the tip of the petal. Fold the ribbon back to the flower centre and catch the ribbon again in the same way. Repeat this procedure, gradually working around in a circle until the outer row of petals is complete. Remember that, as the flower is tilted away from you to give a three dimensional effect, so the petals at the back will be shorter than those in the foreground.

Work a second layer of petals: these will lie between those already formed and be smaller than the first round.

Work the lower poinsettia flower in the same way but make it slightly larger than the top one.

Fir cones: These are worked in brown ribbon and stitched with two strands of brown stranded cotton. Begin by marking an oval shape with tacking stitches for each cone, noting that the cones overlap the wide silver lamé ribbon. Lay the end of the brown ribbon down the centre of the oval, bring the brown thread up at the tip of the oval and encircle the ribbon and take the needle down at the opposite edge of the ribbon, allowing the ribbon to lie flat. Fold the ribbon over the stitch and take it to the opposite edge of the oval shape and repeat the stitch, following the outline of the cone (see fig. 1). Keep folding the ribbon and catching it with a stitch until the cone shape is completely filled with ribbon. Take the ribbon through to the back of the work.

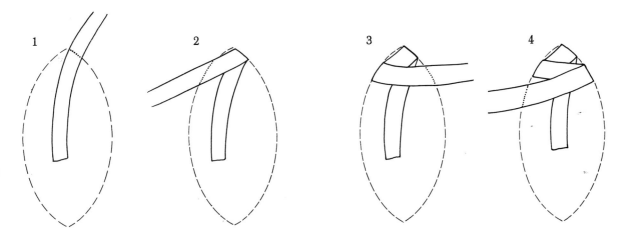

FIGURE 1 *Folding of the ribbon and stitching for a fir cone*

Ribbon French knots: Thread the tapestry needle with dark green ribbon and work two or three French knots at the base of each cone. Ribbon French knots are worked in exactly the same way as the thread ones (see Stitching, page 118).

Poinsettia stems: Using dark green ribbon in the tapestry needle, work long straight stitches to represent the stems.

EMBROIDERY

See Stitching, page 115, for instructions on how to work the stitches.

Bottom holly leaves: Work the vein of each leaf in backstitch – notice the leaves curve upwards – then mark the outline of each leaf in back stitch. If you do not feel confident to stitch without a guideline, trace the outline of the leaves from the photograph and cut these out to give you templates to stitch around.

Working from outside the back stitched outline, satin stitch with two strands of the dark green thread, each stitch being at a sharp angle to the stem. Leave an area either side of the vein unstitched so that this can be filled with stitches at the same sharp angle using the medium green thread.

Top holly leaves: Work these similarly to the bottom leaves, only this time use dark green thread just for the back stitched centre veins and branching veins. Use mid green thread to outline the leaves in back stitch and to

work the outer satin stitch. Fill in close to the veins with the pale green thread.

Feathery foliage: Using dark green thread, back stitch the centre stem and work straight stitches at a sharp angle to the stem to make the spines.

BEADING

See Stitching, page 115.

Poinsettias: Using the beading needle, make a circle of gold beads, and fill the centre with green beads.

Holly berries: Using the beading needle, work groups of red beads with one black bead in the centre of each group. Position the berries where the spaces allow. Use your eye to decide where to place extra leaves and berries to fill out your design.

FINISHING AND MAKING UP

Place the Vilene centrally behind your stitching and attach it around the outside of the design with a row of running stitches so that it will not show when the card is made up.

Quilting: We quilted the card in the photograph by stitching the silver lamé ribbon with silver thread in lines that follow the outer contours of the design (see Stitching, page 115).

See Presentation, page 121, for instructions on how to make up the card.

Flower Splendour

GATHERED RIBBON FLOWERS, STITCHED RIBBON AND
NEEDLEPOINT EMBROIDERY ON CANVAS

A variety of ribbon embroidery flowers surrounded by cleverly shaded rows of mosaic
stitch combine to give this stunning panel a painted quality.   Dominating the
picture are large adjoining daisy-like ribbon flowers with centres of white French
knots and gold beads, surrounded by groups of delicate orange, yellow and white
gathered petal flowers and spikes. The entire background is worked in mosaic stitch
in five shades, specifically chosen to give the picture luminescence, and to add
strength to the flower arrangement.

Only the main flowers and the leaf positions are marked on the template – the smaller flowers are added where you feel they are needed. This way everyone's picture will be slightly different. The outline of the template indicates the finished design size; you can, of course, add more background to make the stitch area larger if you wish.

Materials

- Single canvas 18-count, 8¼ x 6in (21 x 15cm)

  OFFRAY DOUBLE-FACE SATIN RIBBON:
  1.5mm Willow (green) 563, 39in (1m)
           Indian orange 2205, 2¼yd (2m)
           Iris (deeper mauve) 447, 2¼yd (2m)
           Light orchid 430, 2¼yd (2m)
           Baby maize (pale yellow) 617, 39in (1m)
  3mm Cream 815, 39in (1m)
           Yellow gold 660, 20in (50cm)
- Beadesign beads, one packet of gold 72

  ANCHOR STRANDED COTTON (FLOSS),
  ONE SKEIN EACH OF:

Deep yellow 0744	Deep green 263
Cream 926	Pale mauve 342
Pale green 264	Mid mauve 109
Mid green 266	Deep mauve 111

- Vilene extra heavy interfacing 6 x 4in (15x 10cm)

Equipment

- Embroidery frame, 8¼ x 6in (21 x 15cm) or 10in (25cm) circular
- No. 24 tapestry needle
- No. 7 embroidery needle for the gathered flowers
- Beading needle
- Embroidery scissors

PREPARATION

Stretch the fabric tightly in the circular frame or attach it to the rectangular frame with staples or drawing pins (see pages 14 and 16). If you use pins, cover them with masking tape to stop threads catching on them. Using the template provided, mark the position of the two large oval flowers, the tall flowers indicated by a dotted line and the approximate leaf position following the instructions on page 16.

STITCHING

RIBBON EMBROIDERY

See Working with Ribbon, page 11. Follow the template on page 100 carefully and refer often to the photograph opposite for positioning the ribbons.

Mauve stitched flowers: Thread the ribbon into the needle and stitch with it as if it were an ordinary thread. Using the pale mauve ribbon, work the underneath petals of the two large flowers in straight stitches; remember to vary the lengths of the petals and take them outside your drawn oval shapes. The two flowers merge together at the top, so work the back flower first. As you pull the ribbon through, place your finger under the ribbon loop – this helps the ribbon to lie flat. Remember, each petal should point towards the centre of the flower.

With the deeper mauve ribbon, work a second row of stitches over the first row (these will be slightly longer) ensuring that part of the pale under layer shows through. Leave an oval space in the middle to work the flower centre, using the pale yellow 3mm ribbon to work French knots. Ribbon French knots are worked in exactly the same way as the thread ones (see Stitching, page 118).

Tall gathered ribbon flowers: Use the deep yellow 3mm ribbon for the centre flower and cream for the two side ones.

Foliage: With a green thread, mark the central vein of the leaves with a row of back stitch. Using the green ribbon, work a straight stitch at the tip of the leaf about ⅜in (1cm) long and in line with the vein. Then stitch alternately from just outside the outline of the leaf diagonally to the central vein, covering the line of stitching. Each new stitch will cross over the preceding stitch at the line of the central vein.

Small orange flowers: Fit these in the spaces surrounding the main flowers and leaves. Each is made up of seven small stitches worked into one central hole.

BEADING

See Stitching, page 115. Using the beading needle, add a few gold beads to the centres of the mauve flowers and one in the centre of each small orange flower.

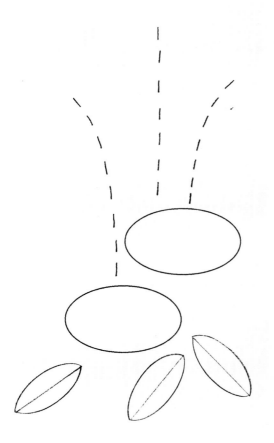

TEMPLATE *for Flower Splendour*

EMBROIDERY

See Stitching, page 115, for instructions on how to work the stitches.

Tall gathered ribbon flowers: Work French knots in matching thread, using all six strands, down the length of the flowers in the spaces between the ribbons.

Using two strands of the palest green thread, work small diagonal stitches around the tall flowers, stitching from the outside in towards the stem.

Background: Using four strands of stranded cotton (floss) throughout, work bands of mosaic stitch following the contour of the design. Start with the deepest green for the first round working complete stitches. Fill any areas of canvas that are too small for a complete mosaic stitch with tent stitch. Fill in any spaces around the ribbon flowers and in between the petals with the deep green using tent stitch.

For the top of the picture continue as follows:

BAND 2: One row in two strands of the deepest green and two strands of medium green;

BAND 3: Four strands of mid green;

BAND 4: Two strands each of mid green and pale green;

BAND 5: Four strands of pale green:

BAND 6: Two strands each of pale green and pale mauve;

BAND 7: Four strands of pale mauve;

BAND 8: Two strands of pale mauve and two strands of medium mauve;

BAND 9: Four strands of medium mauve;

BAND 10: Two strands of medium mauve and two strands of deep mauve;

BAND 11: Four strands of deep mauve;

For the bottom of the picture, work Bands 1 and 2, then after Band 3 complete the areas below the leaves in mid green.

FINISHING AND MAKING UP

See Presentation, page 121, for stretching, mounting and framing the picture. The depth of ribbon embroidery makes it advisable to use a double mount to ensure that the ribbon is not squashed flat by the glass.

Evening Outfit

STITCHED RIBBON, EMBROIDERY AND BEADING

Classic elegance and sophistication are the hallmarks of these black and gold creations. The waistcoat is sumptuously embroidered with gold ribbons and beads in a dramatic design based on circles. The bag, beautifully embroidered with gold on black, and just a hint of pearl, will add sparkle to any occasion.

The Waistcoat

Distinctively glamorous, this waistcoat is actually made from a deceptively straightforward and simple design. If you prefer, apply the design to a commercial pattern.

Materials

- Fabric Flair Jobelan evenweave fabric 28-count in black, 54in (140cm) wide, 1yd (92cm)
- Lining fabric in black, 54in wide, 1yd (92cm)
- Panda polyester lamé ribbon, gold 1, 3mm wide, 5yd (4.6m)
- Panda polyester lamé ribbon, gold 1, 35mm wide, 9yd (8.3m)
- Kreinik metallics ⅛in ribbon, gold 002, two reels
- Kreinik metallics ¹⁄₁₆in ribbon, gold 002, two reels
- Gütermann sewing thread; one reel each of: gold 265; black 000
- Beadesign beads, one packet of pearl 2, three packets of gold 72
- Small gold sequins

Equipment

- Embroidery frame, 22 x 14in (56 x 35.5cm)
- No. 24 tapestry needle for stitching with the Kreinik ribbon
- No. 7 embroidery needle for gathered ribbons
- Beading needle
- Embroidery scissors
- Sewing machine
- Tracing paper and sharp pencil

PATTERN FOR THE WAISTCOAT

The waistcoat was made from a very simple pattern for approximately 34–36in (86–92cm) bust measurement. In this size of book the pattern templates can only be reproduced for the top sections of the front and back pieces (see patterns 1 and 2 on pages 106 and 107). To make the full-size pattern, simply add a rectangle 12½ x 8in (32 x 20cm) to the front, and 12½ x 7½in (32 x 19cm) to the back, at the lower edges where indicated.

As some of the seams are bound, the pattern is marked NTA where no turnings are needed. The double lines on the front pattern show the approximate position for the withdrawal of threads.

For the side gusset patterns, draw two rectangles: one 8½ x 7¾in (21.5 x 197cm) for the evenweave fabric; one 9½ x 7¾in (24 x 197cm) for the lining.

If you decide to use a commercial pattern do avoid one with too many curves as, of course, the ribbons through the withdrawn threads hang as straight lines.

PREPARATION

Trace the pattern, add the extra rectangles needed to make into a full-size pattern, then adapt to your size. If in doubt, cut the pattern out of scrap fabric and tack (baste) the pieces together, so that any alterations to the pattern pieces can be made at this stage before cutting the evenweave or the lining fabric.

As the evenweave fabric tends to fray easily, the embroidery on the front panels in the example was worked on rectangular pieces of fabric in an embroidery frame; the threads were withdrawn but nothing was cut out until the embroidered panels were complete.

Cut two pieces of evenweave fabric, each $22\frac{1}{8}$ x 14in (56 x 35.5cm), cutting carefully along the straight grain, for the two front panels. Stretch one piece for the left front on to the embroidery frame and secure with either staples or drawing pins (see page 14). If you use pins cover the heads with masking tape to stop threads catching on them.

Using the traced pattern, mark the double line for the withdrawal of the threads nearest the front edge: withdraw five threads, leave thirty five threads and withdraw the next five threads. Thread a length of narrow gold Panda ribbon through the space where the threads have been withdrawn, taking it under eight threads and over eight threads alternately.

STITCHING

RIBBON EMBROIDERY AND BEADING

See Working with Ribbon, page 11; also, Stitching, page 115 for hints on beading. Refer often to the photograph on page 104 for position of the ribbons. Trace the template on page 105 and mark the centres of the flower shapes on the fabric following the instructions on page 16.

Gathered ribbon centres: For the full circles, use five gathered ribbons to make the small circle in the middle and, for the half circles, use three gathered ribbons in a semi-circle.

Beading: Using the beading needle, fill the centres with pearl and gold beads. The bead spikes radiate out from the centre; these consist of three gold beads which are threaded on to the beading needle and attached with just one stitch.

Straight stitches: Threading the tapestry needle with the $\frac{1}{16}$in Kreinik ribbon, work a circle of straight

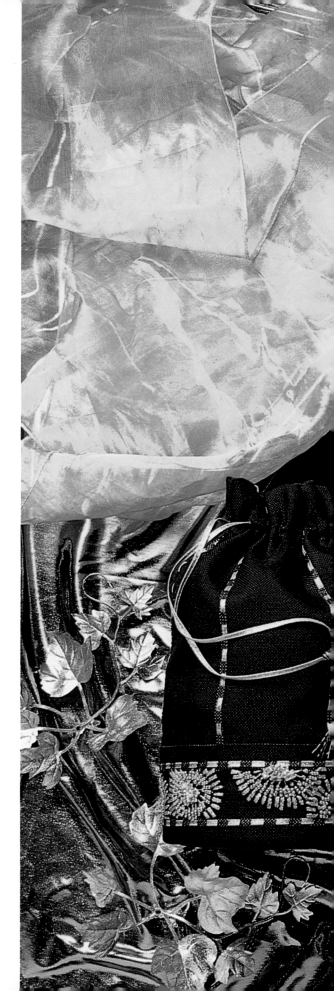

stitches radiating out from the bead spikes and then a further row in the same way with the ¹⁄₈in Kreinik ribbon.

Sequins: Apply groups of three sequins between the embroidered motifs, with a gold bead to attach each one. Using the beading needle and gold sewing thread, come up through the sequin, through the bead and back down through the sequin and the fabric and fasten securely.

Place the traced pattern on to the fabric, matching up the withdrawn thread lines, and tack (baste) around the shape, allowing ¹⁄₂in (1.25cm) turnings where indicated. Take the fabric from the frame and cut out.

Stretch the second piece of evenweave fabric on to the frame and repeat the entire procedure for the right front, reversing the pattern to obtain the position of the double line for the withdrawal of threads and reversing the embroidery tracing.

FINISHING AND MAKING UP

Cut out the rest of the pattern pieces in evenweave fabric, placing the fabric fold to the centre of the back and noting where seam allowances are to be added. Join the back and two fronts at the shoulder seams. Press.

Lining: In the same way, cut out all the lining fabric pieces, allowing for seams where indicated. Join the back and two fronts at the shoulder seams and press.

With wrong sides together, put the lining inside the outer waistcoat and tack (baste) together, stitching from the lower edge of the right front up, round the neck and back down the left front. Also tack (baste) the long side edges together – to each other, not front to back.

Side panels gussets: Tack (baste) the side gussets together in pairs, evenweave to lining fabric, wrong sides together, leaving ¹⁄₂in (1.25cm) of lining fabric extending each side. Bind the top edge with the wide gold ribbon, folding it in half and using it flat. Stitch close to the edge of the ribbon with the gold sewing thread. Fold the excess lining fabric over the evenweave fabric to the outside and zigzag in place.

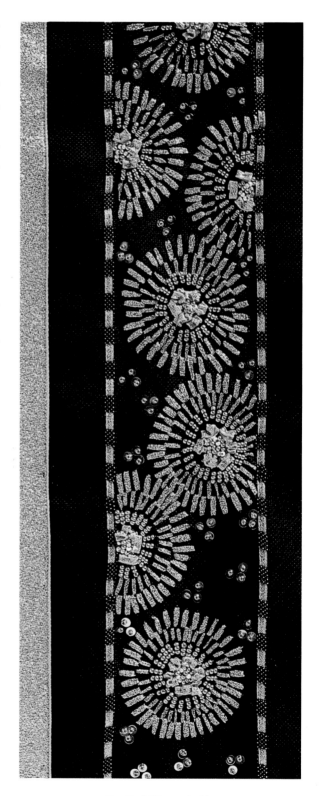

Detail of ribbon embroidery

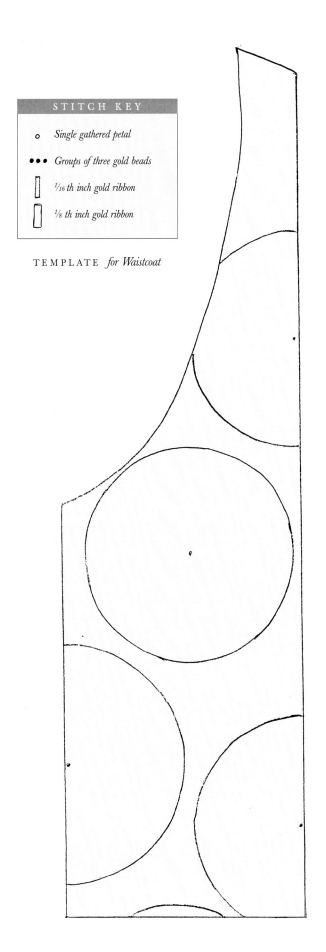

○   *Single gathered petal*

••• *Groups of three gold beads*

▯   *¹⁄₁₆ th inch gold ribbon*

▯   *¹⁄₈ th inch gold ribbon*

TEMPLATE *for Waistcoat*

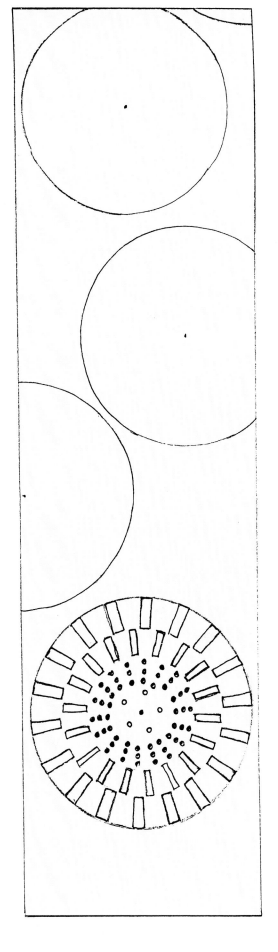

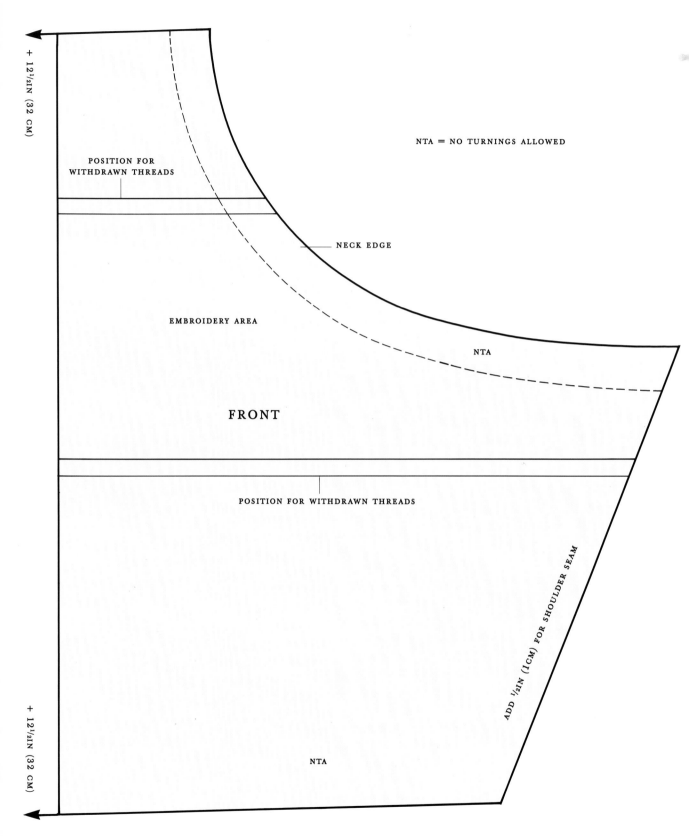

+ 12¹/₂IN (32 CM)

POSITION FOR
WITHDRAWN THREADS

NTA = NO TURNINGS ALLOWED

NECK EDGE

EMBROIDERY AREA

NTA

FRONT

POSITION FOR WITHDRAWN THREADS

ADD ¹/₂IN (1CM) FOR SHOULDER SEAM

+ 12¹/₂IN (32 CM)

NTA

PATTERN 1 *Front Waistcoat*

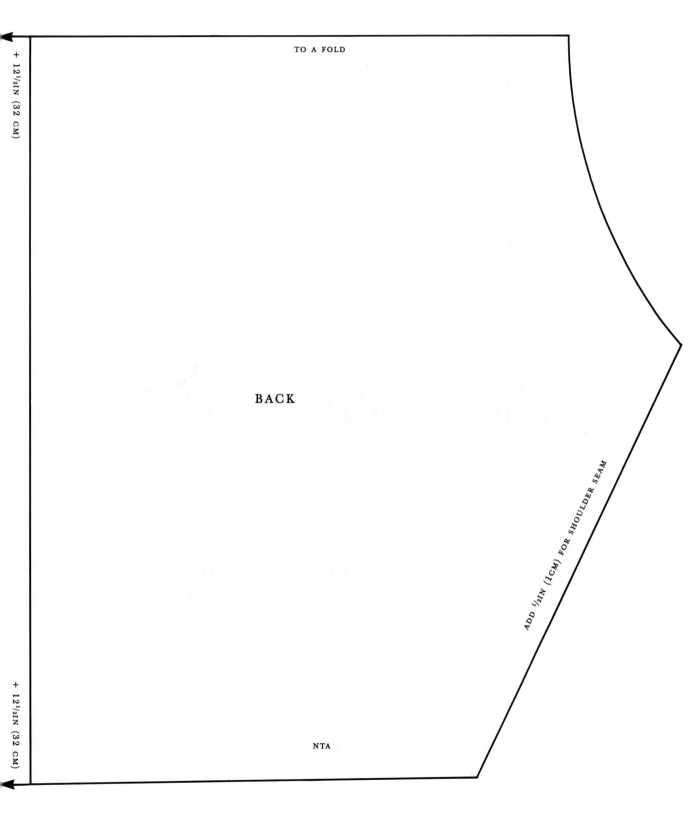

TO A FOLD

BACK

ADD ¹⁄₂IN (1CM) FOR SHOULDER SEAM

NTA

PATTERN 2 *Back Waistcoat*

Zigzag stitch all round the tacked edges at the front, neck and sides to give added strength. Bind the neck edge with the wide gold ribbon. Bind the shoulder/side edges, working from the front lower edge, up over the shoulder and down to the back lower edge.

Insert one side panel by laying it under the bound edges of the main section, matching the lower edges of the front and back. Machine together on the folded edge of the ribbon binding. On the inside, handstitch the gusset sides to the waistcoat. Repeat with the other side.

Bottom band: Cut a length of evenweave fabric 45 x 3in (114 x 7.5cm) and a length of lining fabric 45 x 4in (114 x 10cm). Lay these pieces wrong sides together, matching the lower edges, and bind the lower edge with the wide gold ribbon. At the top edge, fold the excess lining fabric over to the right side and zigzag ¼in (6mm) from the edge and trim.

With wide gold ribbon, bind right across the lower edge of the waistcoat, across the right front, side gusset, back, side gusset and left front. Lay the bound lower edge on top of the prepared band and tack (baste) carefully together, ensuring that the top edge of the band will be caught when the ribbon edge is stitched. Machine along the edge of the ribbon binding and also along the fold of the ribbon binding.

Lay, pin and tack (baste) wide gold ribbon binding on the two front edges, turning in the ends neatly. Machine close to the ribbon edges. Fold the ribbon in half and turn to the inside. Hem in place by hand.

Press well with a warm iron.

The Bag

Perfect with the matching waistcoat, the bag is roomy enough to hold everything you might need.

PREPARATION

Cut three pieces of evenweave fabric as follows, cutting the rectangular pieces exactly along the threads:

Materials

- Fabric Flair Jobelan evenweave 28-count fabric, 54in (140cm) wide, 12 x 54in (30 x 140cm)
- Lining fabric in black, 18in (46cm)
- Wadding (batting), 8in (20cm) square
- Gütermann sewing thread in black, one reel
- Small amount of Coton à Broder in gold and black for the tassels
- Panda polyester lamé ribbon, gold 1, 3mm wide, 7yd (6.5m)
- Kreinik metallic Balger ⅛in ribbon, gold 002, one reel
- Madeira metallic No. 12, gold 33, one reel
- Beadesign beads, two packets of gold 72, one packet of pearl 2
- Greyboard or similar, 2mm thick, cut into: two circles each 5½in (14cm) diameter; one length 2½ x 20in (6.5 x 51cm)

Equipment

- Embroidery frame, 22 x 9in (56 x 23cm)
- No. 7 embroidery needle
- Large-eyed needle for threading ribbon through channel
- Beading needle
- Curved needle
- Embroidery scissors
- Sewing machine

20½ x 9in (52 x 23cm); 20½ x 4½in (52 x 11.5cm); 7½in (19cm) diameter circle.

Cut three pieces of lining fabric to the following dimensions:

20½ x 8in (52.25 x 20cm); 20½ x 4½in (52.25 x 11.5cm); 7½in (19cm) diameter circle.

Tack (baste) strips of cotton fabric on to the long narrow strip of evenweave fabric to make it large enough to fit the frame. This fabric will fray, so do not stitch too near to the edge. Stretch this on to the embroidery frame and secure with either staples or drawing pins (see page 14). If you use pins cover the heads with masking tape to stop threads catching.

Moulding card: Position a block of wood or similar between the two circles of card so that they are spaced approximately 1½in (4cm) apart (see fig. 1). Using a damp sponge and a stroking action, wet one side of the long length of thick card until this can be gently moulded around the card circles – the ends will overlap slightly to allow for trimming later. Secure with string or elastic bands and leave for several hours (preferably overnight) to completely dry out. Remove the elastic bands and block.

STITCHING

Run a gathering thread round the edge of the circle of lining fabric, lay one of the card circles on top and pull up the gathers. Lace from side to side all round the circle, using black sewing thread double. Repeat this procedure and cover the second circle with evenweave

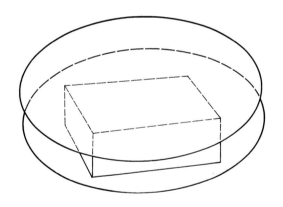

FIGURE 1   *Creating pattern for moulding card*

fabric, this time positioning a circle of wadding (batting) between the fabric and the card before gathering and lacing.

Put the moulded card around the covered circles and trim so that the edges butt together. Join securely with masking tape.

Place the long narrow strip of lining fabric round the moulded card and pin tightly; remove the lining from the moulded card and stitch the seam, trimming the surplus. Place inside the moulded card, wrong side to

the card, fold and stretch the fabric out over the moulded card at the top and bottom. Lace the edges together on the outside.

Drawn threads and threaded ribbon: Lay the piece of evenweave fabric for the main part of the bag flat on a table and, starting about twelve threads from the right-hand edge, withdraw one thread across the narrow width. Then remove four more (making five in all). Thread a piece of lamé ribbon through the spaces from which the threads have been withdrawn, passing it over eight threads and under eight alternately. Count thirty five threads and then withdraw the next five and insert the lamé ribbon as before. Repeat this procedure across the fabric until you have seven ribbons woven into the fabric. Measure around the outside of the covered card tube and seam the threaded fabric to that measurement; seam the lining fabric in the same way. Press the seams.

Place the lining fabric tube inside the evenweave fabric tube, right sides together and seam along the top edge, pressing the turnings towards the evenweave fabric and stitching them back. Turn the lining to the inside and fold down the outside fabric so that there is 1¼in (3cm) of evenweave fabric folded to the inside.

Draw-string channel: Stitching through both fabrics, machine a line of stitching on the seam line and another just over ½in (1.25cm) below.

EMBROIDERY AND BEADING FOR THE LOWER BAND

See Working with Ribbon, page 11; also, Stitching, page 115, for hints on beading. Refer to the evening bag flower template on page 110 and to the photograph of the finished piece on page 102–103 for position of the ribbons and beads.

Tack (baste) around an area 2½ x 18¾in (6.5 x 47.5cm) for the embroidery, making sure that you are stitching exactly along the line of the threads. Measure ½in (1.25cm) in from one long side and withdraw a thread from the fabric, followed by four more threads. Thread a length of narrow ribbon through as before and

STITCH KEY

○	*Single gathered petal*	●—	*Long armed French knot*
●●●	*Groups of three gold beads*	▭	*Kreinik ribbon stitches*

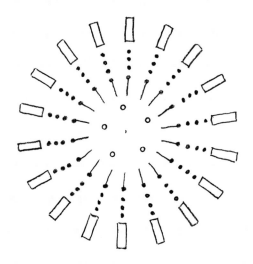

TEMPLATE *for Evening Bag flower*

do the same along the other edge, leaving a strip of fabric between the ribbons for the embroidery.

Full flowers: From the tacking line at one of the narrow ends, measure 3in (7.5cm) and put in a pin; place pins also at 9in (23cm) and 15in (38cm), marking the positions for the three full flower shapes. Make a circle of five gathered ribbons at each of these points.

Half flowers: Measure 2in (5cm) from the ribbon circle and place a pin on one of the long tacked edges. Measure a further 2in (5cm) and this time put a pin on the other edge. Continue doing this until you have pins in position to mark the six half flower shapes. Make semi-circle centres with three gathered ribbons at each pin mark.

Long-armed French knots: Surround each ribbon group with long-armed French knots worked with the Madeira metallic gold thread.

Beading: Using the beading needle, fill the centres of the half flowers and full flowers with pearl and gold beads. The bead spikes radiate out from the centre; these consist of three gold beads which are threaded on to the beading needle and attached with just one stitch.

Straight stitches: Thread the tapestry needle with the Kreinik ribbon and work arcs of straight stitches radiating out from the bead spikes.

FINISHING AND MAKING UP

Cut the embroidery from the frame, allowing 1¼in (3cm) all round. Join the ends of the band and lay one edge of the face of the embroidery to the right side of the lower edge of upper section of the bag tube, tack (baste) and machine round the bottom edge. Fold the embroidery down and under the lower edge.

From the inside of the bag, pull up the edge of the embroidered fabric, tack and push in the fabric-covered circular base from below. Ladder stitch the circular base securely into position using a curved needle. From the inside, remove the tacking (basting) thread, flatten down all the turnings and push the lining-covered circular base into place, lacing side down.

Draw-strings: Thread a length of gold ribbon measuring 27in (69cm) through the channel, starting ¼in (6mm) in from the seam on one side and going round the top of the bag and out ¼in (6mm) the other side of the seam. Join the ends and work the ribbon round until the join disappears into the channel. Fold the top of the bag in half to find the opposite side to the seam and thread another similar length of ribbon through the channel, leaving a gap of ½in (1.25cm) between where the ribbon goes in and comes out. Finish this ribbon in the same way. Pull the ribbons up from both sides to close the bag.

Tassels: Make two tassels from the black and gold Coton à Broder and the metallic gold thread – see instructions for how to make tassels for the Needlecase on page 20. Attach these at the half-way mark of the ribbons.

Poppies and Daises

STITCHED RIBBON AND NEEDLEPOINT
EMBROIDERY ON CANVAS

*A spectacular display of searing reds and strong, bright yellows, surrounded by
clear-sky blue – Poppies and Daisies could only have been born of the very height of
summer. The flowers look as if they have been painted in ribbon, rather than
stitched; and the lively, long, smooth stitches contrast effectively with the textured,
regular needlepoint background.*

Pieces such as this give you the opportunity to make your own mark on the design. Place the main flowers accurately, then try working more freely, placing smaller flowers and leaves approximately. Why not add an extra flower, or change the position of some of them? That way your picture will be slightly different.

Materials

- Single canvas 18-count, 17¹/₂in (44.5cm) square

ANCHOR STRANDED COTTON (FLOSS):

One skein	Charcoal grey 236
Two skeins	Green 266
Three skeins	Cream 386
	Palest green 264
	Mid green 267
	Palest mauve 117
	Mid mauve 118
	Deep mauve 119
Four skeins	Deepest green 268

PANDA DOUBLE SATIN RIBBON:

1.5 mm	Red 355	10yd (9m)
3 mm	Red 387	5¹/₂yd (5m)
	Orange 310	3¹/₂yd (3m)
	White 235	5¹/₂yd (5m)
	Pale blue 162	4¹/₂yd (4m)
	Deep yellow 409	5¹/₂yd (5m)
	Mauve 262	7³/₄yd (7m)
	Pale green 257	4¹/₂yd (4m)

- Beadesign beads in gold 72 and black 78

Equipment

- Embroidery frame, 17¹/₂in (44.5cm) square
- No. 24 tapestry needle for the canvas work
- No. 7 embroidery needle for the ribbon work
- Beading needle
- Embroidery scissors

PREPARATION

Stretch the canvas on to the embroidery frame. Secure with either staples or drawing pins (see page 14). If you use pins cover the heads with masking tape to stop threads catching on them.

Trace the template on page 114 and transfer the design to the fabric (see page 16 for instructions).

STITCHING

RIBBON EMBROIDERY

See Working with Ribbon, page 11. Refer often to the photograph on page 112 for colour and position of the ribbon.

Poppies: Using red 1.5mm ribbon as a thread, work from ¹/₈in (3mm) outside the outline of the poppies, making irregular straight stitches. Each stitch should point to the centre of the flower. Then use the second red ribbon, 3mm wide, and work a second row of

stitches, integrating them with the first row. Gradually work towards the centre of the flower with the 3mm red ribbon. Work the last round with orange ribbon to complete the petals.

Large daisies: Work fans of white ribbon in straight stitches. Using pale blue ribbon, work stitches in between the white ones as shown by the dotted lines in fig. 1. Work the centres in yellow ribbon French knots. Ribbon French knots are worked in exactly the same way as the thread ones (see Stitching, page 118).

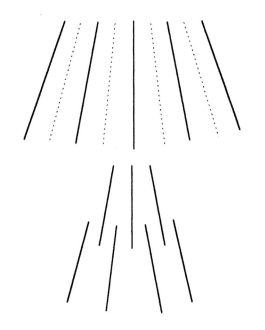

FIGURE 1 *Straight stitch arrangement for the white and blue daisies (above) and the mauve flowers (below)*

Small yellow flowers: Work short straight stitches in yellow ribbon, leaving an oval for the centre and making the back petals slightly shorter than those in the foreground.

Mauve flowers: Start at the top of each shape with a fan of three straight stitches in mauve ribbon, then add a second row in between (see fig. 1). Try to avoid leaving gaps. Continue to work in this way until the flower is complete.

Veins of the leaves: Couch pale green ribbon in curves along the surface of the leaves.

Flower stems: Work straight stitches in pale green ribbon.

EMBROIDERY

See Stitching, page 115, for instructions on how to work the stitches. Use six strands of stranded cotton (floss) to work all the background and leaves.

Poppies: Using all six strands of stranded cotton (floss), work long-armed French knots in charcoal grey. Vary the lengths of the stitches.

Small yellow flowers: Fill with cream thread French knots, using all six strands.

Leaves: Using the palest green thread, work the outline of all the leaves in mosaic stitch. Fill leaves 1 and 2 with tent stitch in deepest green. Work leaves 3 and 4 in mosaic stitch in mid green. Work leaves 5, 6 and 7 in mosaic stitch in palest green. Where there is insufficient space for a mosaic stitch, fill in with tent stitches.

BEADING

See Stitching, page 115.

Poppies: Add small black beads as in the illustration.

Large daisies: Add gold beads to the centres.

Small yellow flowers: Work an oval of gold beads close to the petal ends.

BACKGROUND CANVAS WORK

The base of the picture: Following the outline of the leaves, and changing colour as you work towards the bottom, work rounds of mosaic stitches as follows:

ROUND 1: Six strands of mid mauve.

ROUND 2: Three strands of mid mauve and three strands of deep mauve.

ROUND 3: Six strands of deep mauve.

ROUND 4: Three strands of deep mauve and three strands of deepest green.

ROUND 5: Six strands of deepest green.

Fill in with mosaic stitch to make the bottom and sides straight.

The top of the picture: Work in bands of mosaic stitch, working from the outside towards the centre as follows:

BAND 1: One row in three strands of deepest green and three strands of deep mauve.

BAND 2: Three rows in three strands of deep mauve and three strands of mid mauve.

BAND 3: One row in six strands of cream.

BAND 4: Three rows in three strands of mid mauve and three strands of palest mauve.

BAND 5: Five rows in three strands of palest mauve and three strands of palest green.

BAND 6: Five rows in three strands of palest green and three strands of cream .

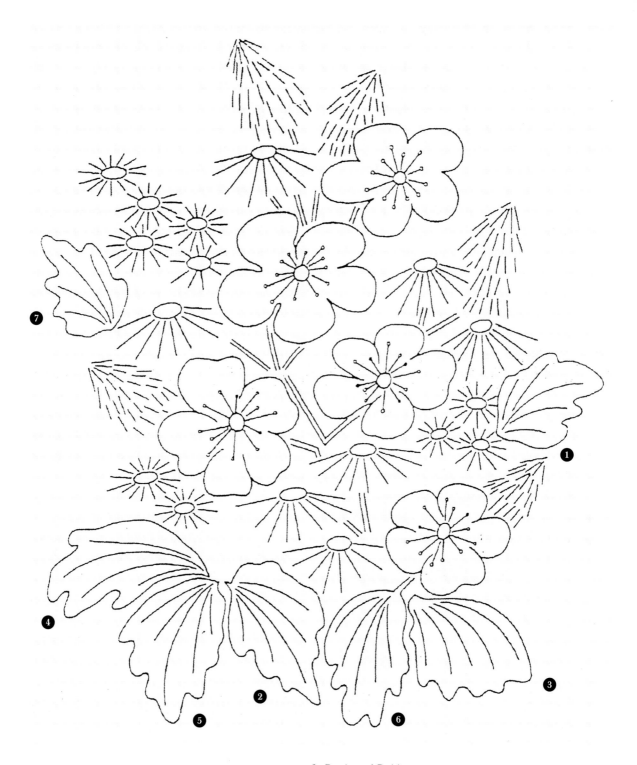

TEMPLATE *for Poppies and Daisies*

Behind the red poppies work an area in greens, some in mosaic stitch and some in tent stitch. You will need to work between the ribbon petals in some of the flowers. Finally, work the remaining area in cream. Keep referring to the photograph throughout and, at the end, check carefully to see that all the canvas is covered.

FINISHING AND MAKING UP

See Presentation, page 121, for stretching, mounting and framing the picture. You will need to use two mounts because the beaded flower centres stand out from the stitching.

Stitching

WORKING FROM A CHART

Our charts for counted thread embroidery are simple to follow. Each square on the chart represents either one block of an evenweave such as Aida, or one intersection of the warp and weft threads of an evenweave such as linen. On cross stitch charts each square represents one cross stitch; thick lines represent back stitch; dots represent French knots. Colours are shown by different symbols.

As a general rule, start stitching from the centre of the design. To find the centre of your fabric, tack (baste) a vertical and a horizontal line across the middle, in a light coloured thread. Some projects start at a different point which you find by counting threads.

LETTERING

To work out the area required for a name, draw the letters out on graph paper first and arrange them to fit the space. Alternatively, using the charted alphabets provided, total the number of stitches in the width of each letter, plus spaces, and divide this by two to find the centre of the word and start stitching from this point on the fabric. Remember to check that the finished name will fit into the space available; if necessary, adjust the spaces between the individual letters.

QUILTING

This is a way of joining two pieces of fabric together, usually over padded interlining. The quilting method we use is a simple lines of back stitch, taking the needle through the embroidered fabric and the interfacing. This gives an interesting textured background, and helps with the final stretching. The quilting could also be worked using a sewing machine: it would be necessary to leave the embroidery tightly stretched in the frame, tacking the interfacing to the back of the work before starting to stitch. Remove the presser foot and drop the feed teeth to prepare for free-machining, so that you are in control of the size of the stitch.

BLACKWORK

For the simple blackwork designs used in this book, the order in which the stitches are carried out is not important as long as it is consistent. Use a back stitch and follow the charts provided, remembering to try to avoid carrying the thread across large open areas of the back of the fabric where it might show through on the front. There are many books which show a variety of different blackwork stitches and these could be substituted for the ones shown in the projects.

ATTACHING BEADS

Beads are attached using a matching sewing thread. A very fine needle is required, and special long beading needles are available. However, the authors have found it easier to use a No.10 Betweens/Quilting needle, which is only about 1¼in (3cm) long. Bring the needle up through the fabric, slip the bead (or beads) on to the needle and slide it down the thread, pass the needle back through the same hole in the fabric. If you are attaching several beads at a time, slip them all on to the needle and take it back through the fabric at an appropriate distance from the first hole.

THE STITCH DIRECTORY

COUNTED THREAD AND CANVASWORK STITCHES

To begin stitching on canvas or an evenweave fabric, knot the thread and take the needle from the front down through the fabric, leaving the knot on the surface. When you have covered the threads on the back of the work with stitching, cut off the knots.

Tent stitch: The most common and versatile of the canvaswork stitches as it produces an even texture and can be used in any type of design. A diagonal stitch over a single intersection which can be worked in rows diagonally, horizontally or vertically. When using tent stitch in a single colour over a large area, work in diagonal rows for a smoother effect.

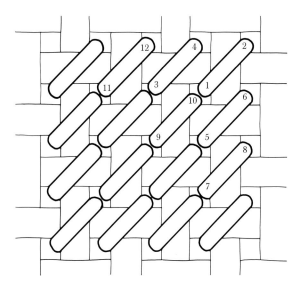

Cross Stitch: Two diagonal stitches at right angles to each other forming an x-shaped cross. The most important thing is always to ensure that the top stitch of every cross in a piece of work always lies in the same direction, as shown in the diagram. Can be worked by completing each cross individually; or in rows, laying all the underneath threads in one direction and then working back along the row putting in the top threads.

Mosaic Stitch: A repeated series of three diagonal stitches, which can be worked in rows diagonally or horizontally. Each complete mosaic stitch consists of three stitches worked diagonally over one intersection, over two and over one. When covering an area of canvas and one row of stitches has been worked, it is easier to turn the canvas through 180° in order to repeat the row in reverse.

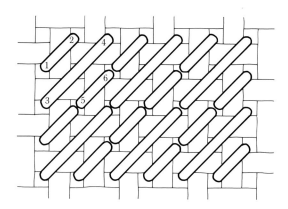

Rice or Crossed Corners Stitch: One large x-shaped cross stitch laid over four intersections of canvas thread each way, the corners of which are then crossed at right angles by a contrasting thread and forming a diamond shape on top of the cross. Work all the large crosses first, ensuring that the second stitch always lies in the same direction, and then the smaller diagonal stitches.

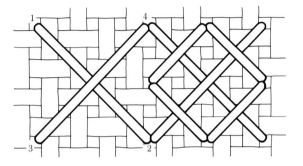

Cushion Stitch: Blocks of stitches forming small cushions which are arranged with the diagonals in alternating directions. Each block can consist of any number of stitches. Complete each series of stitches to form a cushion (e.g. for a block of seven over one intersection, over two, over three, over four, over three, over two and over one, forming a square) before proceeding to the next block. If covering a large area and in different colours, work the blocks in rows according to the desired pattern.

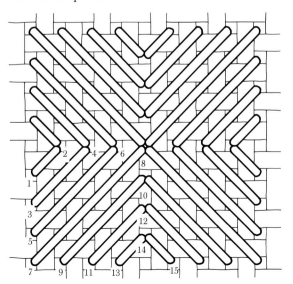

Rhodes Stitch: A densely-worked stitch with a raised centre, covering a square of canvas. Begin by bringing the thread up at position 1 and down at 2, continuing to bring the thread up at the odd numbered squares and down at the even ones in numerical order;. Note that the final stitch repeats the first but brings the thread up at 2 and down at 1.

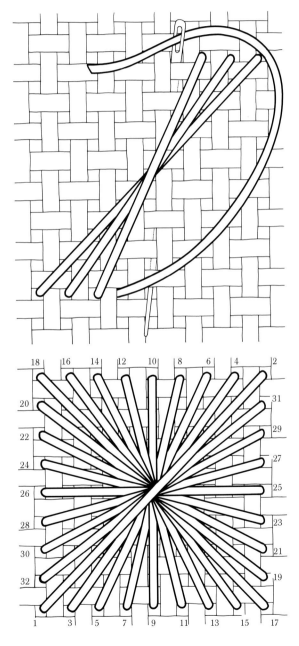

FREEHAND EMBROIDERY STITCHES

Back Stitch: The embroiderers' way of drawing lines on fabric. Bring the thread up through the fabric, take the needle backwards and down through the fabric and bring it up again the same distance in front. Keep the stitches as even as possible.

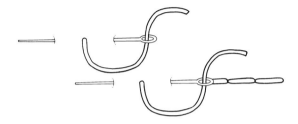

Chain Stitch: The thread forms a loop as a running stitch is made, so forming a chain. The links of the chain should be equal in size.

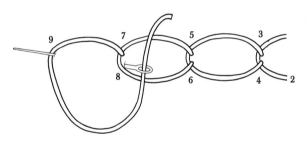

Herringbone Stitch: A series of long diagonal stitches worked between two imaginary lines. Keep the spacing regular and the crossed threads equal in length.

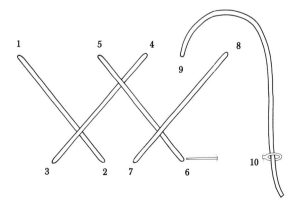

KNOTTED STITCHES

French knot: To produce a knot, bring the thread up through the fabric at the point where the knot is required. Holding the thread with your thumb, loop the thread around the needle once and insert the point into the fabric again immediately beside the starting position and pull the thread through to the back.

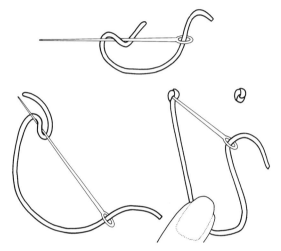

Long-armed French knot: As for the ordinary French knot but bring the needle up through the fabric at the point where the arm of the knot is to be positioned and, after looping the thread around the needle, insert the needle again at the position where the knot is to be formed, pulling the thread through.

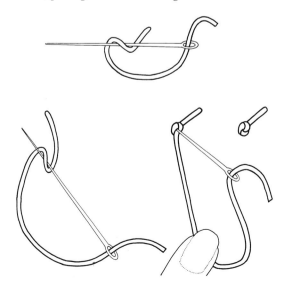

Bullion Stitch: Gives the effect of a coil. Decide on the size of the required Bullion Stitch and make a back stitch in the fabric of that size. Keeping the needle in position, twist the thread around the needle as many times as needed to fill the back stitch space. Hold the coiled thread down as the needle is pulled through and passed back through the fabric at the original point of entry, pulling the thread until the stitch lies flat.

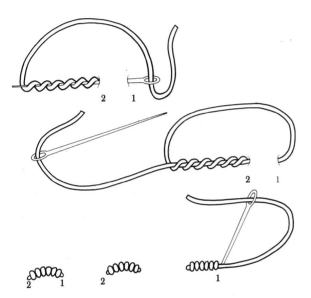

JOINING STITCHES

Ladder Stitch: A way to join two fabric surfaces together invisibly. Make a small stitch in one fabric and one in the fabric to be joined to it at a point immediately opposite to where the needle emerged from the first stitch. In some cases, e.g. box-making, it may help to use a curved needle.

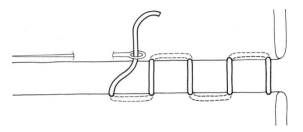

Couching: A method of holding threads, cords, braids, ribbons, and so forth, on the surface of a fabric with stitches in a matching or contrasting thread. Place the ribbon to be couched in its final position and bring the couching thread up through the fabric close beside the ribbon. With small, straight stitches taken over the ribbon at regular intervals along its length, use the thread to hold the ribbon down. Use a large-eyed needle to pass the ends of the ribbon being couched through the fabric; secure these ends to the back of the fabric.

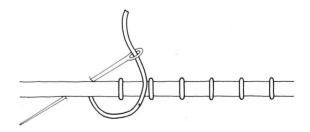

STRETCHING OR BLOCKING

If you have used an embroidery frame, your work should have retained its shape and dimensions well. However, if it has become distorted, the work will require blocking - that is, gently pulling it back into shape. Take great care that you don't damage the ribbon work.

There are two methods: dry-blocking and wet-blocking. Both are done on a blocking board which is made by covering a piece of unfinished board (i.e. neither stained, varnished nor painted) with sheeting, and fastening this to the edges with rust-proof drawing pins.If all the materials used are colourfast and no metal threads are involved then you can wet-block your work. If any materials are non-colourfast or you've used metal threads, then the work must be dry-blocked.

Wet-blocking: Draw an accurate pencil outline of the required finished dimensions on the blocking board, making sure that right angles are accurate. Gently spray the back of the embroidery, making it evenly damp rather than wet. Lay the work, face up, on the blocking board and pin to the marked outline - pin at the top and bottom of the vertical centre first, then to the horizontal and then work outwards from these middle points, pinning at regular ³⁄₄in (2cm) intervals. Allow the work to dry naturally, in a horizontal position, until completely dry, probably 24–48 hours.

Dry-blocking: Block the embroidery in a similar way but do not dampen it. Leave for around 24–48 hours.

LACING

Depending on the piece of work being mounted, accurately cut a piece of backing card or board to the dimensions of the finished piece (checking right angles carefully) and cover this with a natural fabric, interlining or pad with Vilene extra heavy interfacing, as recommended.

Lay the embroidery to be mounted face down - on a piece of foam or soft padding (a folded towel will suffice) to absorb any surface embellishments and position the board carefully on top. Pull and pin the margins of the fabric to the back of the board and check that the embroidery is being held in the correct position before lacing the opposite sides, using light string, thin crochet cotton or similar thread (fig.1). The lacing should be really taut and properly secured. Cut away excess at the corners, mitre carefully (fig.2) and stitch down.

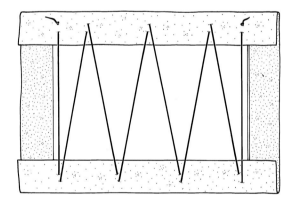

FIGURE 1 *Lacing*

To lace a round or oval piece of work, run a gathering thread around the outer margin of the embroidery and pull this up over the backing board and fasten off; lace across the diameters, gradually working round the circumference.

Once the work has been mounted on the backing board, seal the edges all round with masking tape.

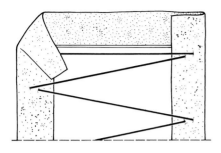

FIRST CORNER FABRIC PULLED DOWN

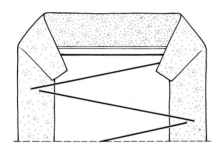

TWO CORNERS HALF MITRED

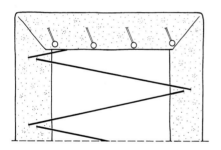

FULL MITRES PINNED IN POSITION

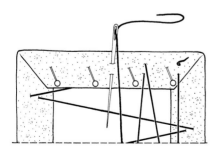

BEGINNING TO LACE

FIGURE 2 *Mitring*

MOUNTS

With few exceptions, work which is to be framed is improved by being placed within a suitable mount. You will get the best advice from a professional framer, particularly one who is used to dealing with embroidered pieces. The professional will advise on the most suitable colour, size and shape of the mount, or the possibility of a using a double mount. Mounting board with a coloured core is also available and provides a subtle thin contrasting line. If you are going to mount your work yourself, for pleasing proportions, position your work so that there is a little more mount at the lower edge than the top. Mount the work onto the mounting board with double-sided tape or white adhesive.

FRAMING

Having put so much time and effort into any piece of work, it is worthwhile seeking the help and advice of a professional, unless you have considerable experience. The choice of the correct framing can make or mar the end product. Always ensure that the glass does not touch the embroidery.

CARDS

There are a host of cards with cut apertures of various shapes on the market today, making it possible to buy nearly any colour and/or size that may be required. Place Vilene extra heavy interfacing, cut ¼in (6mm) larger all round than the size of the aperture, behind the work prior to positioning it in the card, so that it will be raised through the aperture. For neatness, and to avoid the possibility of getting glue on the work, always use double-sided sticky tape to secure the embroidery fabric to the card and also to fix the two faces of the folded card together.

Alphabet Charts

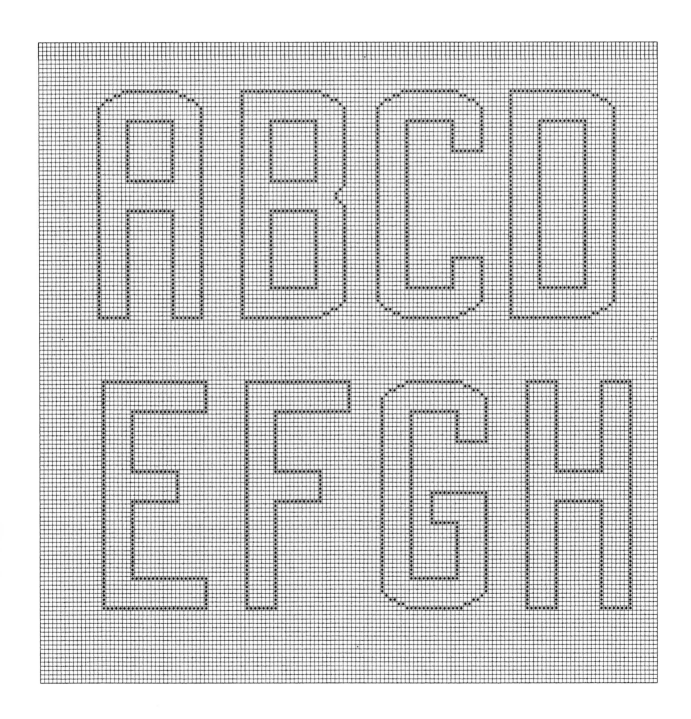

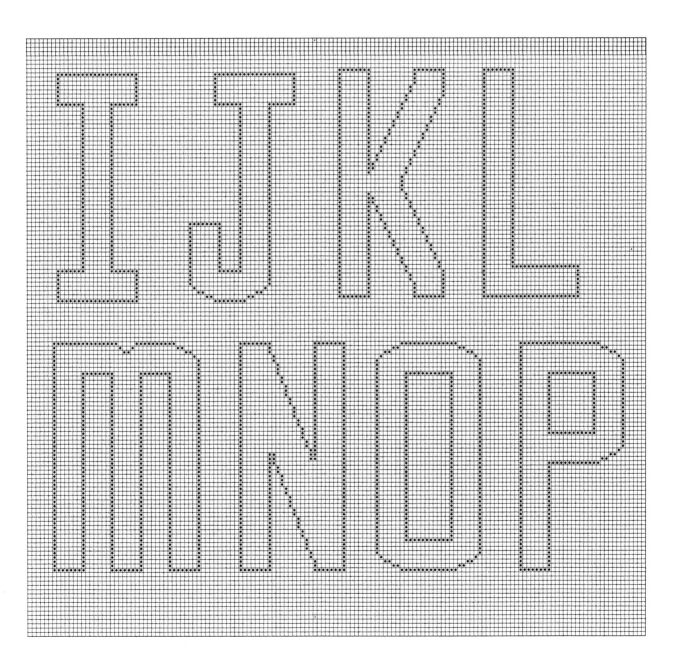

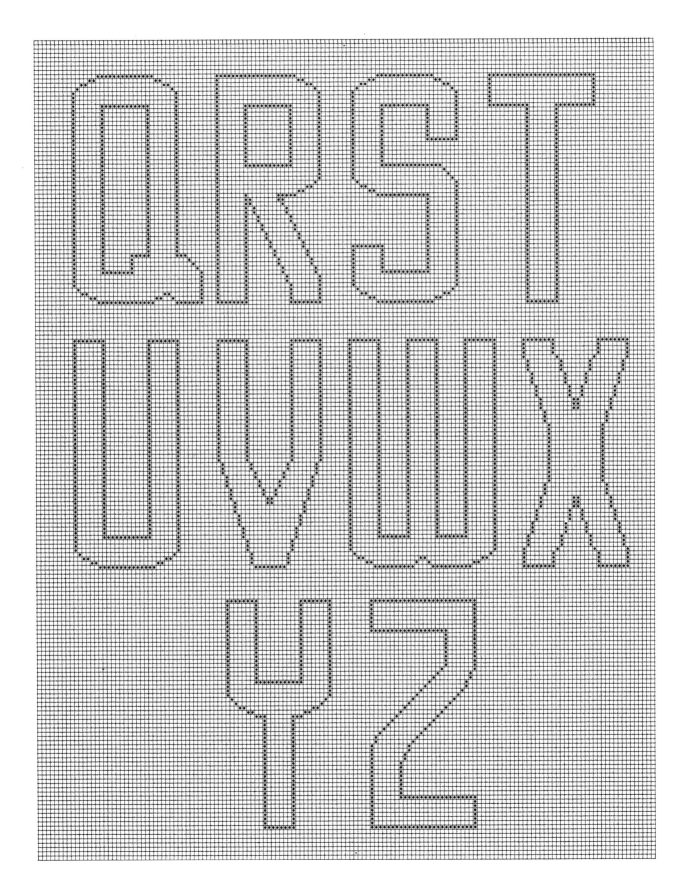

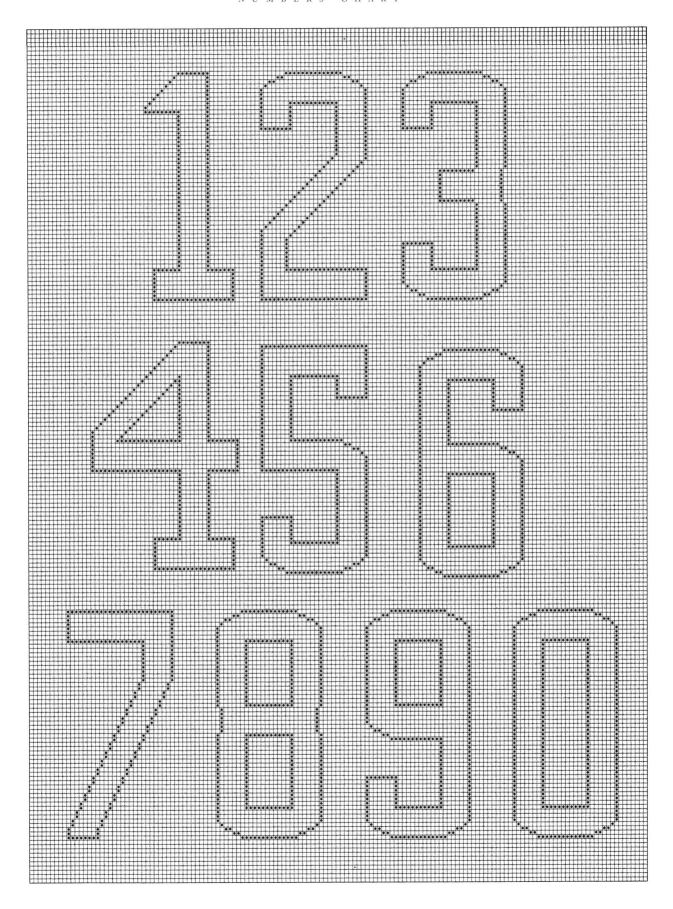

Suppliers and Stockists

BARNYARNS LTD
P O Box 28
THIRSK
N Yorkshire YO7 3YN
Mail order suppliers of threads, fabrics, ribbons, kits & needlework accessories. SAE for catalogue

COATS CRAFTS UK LTD
P O Box 22
The Lingfield Estate
McMullen Road
DARLINGTON
Co. Durham DL1 1YQ
01325 365457
Suppliers of threads, fabrics, ribbons, kits and haberdashery products.

FABRIC FLAIR LTD
The Old Brewery
The Close
WARMINSTER
Wiltshire BA12 9AL
0800 716851
Suppliers of specialist embroidery fabrics

FANTASY FABRICS
Greenmantle
Plough Lane
CHRISTLETON
Chester CH3 7BA
01244 335296
Mail order suppliers of Indian rayon threads, congress cloth, metallic threads, ribbons and fabrics

FRAMECRAFT
MINIATURES LTD
372-376 Summer Lane
Hockley
BIRMINGHAM B19 3QA
Suppliers of frames, paperweights, boxes, cards, dressing table accessories, etc.

DILYS FRONKS
Llain Delyn
New Brighton Road
SYCHDYN
Mold
Clwyd CH7 6EE
Box kits, Etui kits, as well as many patchwork items. Kits distributed by:

PAULINE & ALAN BOLT
Swiss Cottage
Milton Abbas
BLANDFORD
FORUM,
Dorset DT11 0BJ
01258 880852

HARLEQUIN
E A & H M Bull Ltd
MANNINGTREE
Essex CO11 1UX
01206 396167
Use customers' own fabrics for making up waistcoats, bags, ties, belts, wedding accessories and hats.

IMPRESS CARDS & CRAFT
MATERIALS
Slough Farm
Westhall
HALESWORTH
Suffolk IP19 8RN
01986 781422

KERNOW CRAFT
WOODTURNING
The Courtyard Shopping
Mews
9 High Street
ST IVES
Cornwall
01736 793628

MADEIRA THREADS
UK LTD
P O Box 16
THIRSK
North Yorkshire YO7 3YX
Manufacturers of threads, kits, wooden frames, books and suppliers of fabrics and needles.

RIBBON DESIGNS
42 Lake View
EDGWARE
Middlesex HA8 7RU
Suppliers of silk ribbons.

SELECTUS LTD
Biddulph
STOKE ON TRENT
Staffs ST8 7RH
01449 740221
Manufacturers of all types of ribbon. Telephone for further information.

SPOILT FOR CHOICE
35 March Road
Wimblington
MARCH
Cambs PE15 0RW
01354 740341
Mail order suppliers of beads and beadwork kits.

THREADS & SO MUCH
MORE
70½ Roseville Street
ST HELIER
Jersey
Channel Islands
01534 36196
Mail order supplier of threads, fabrics, beads, ribbon and embroidery books.

WILLOW FABRICS
27 Willow Green
KNUTSFORD
Cheshire WA16 6AX

Acknowledgements

*Our grateful thanks go to the following individuals
and companies for their kind co-operation in the compilation of this book:*

SUE ASHBY - for making up the christening robe
and little girl's dress so beautifully.

COATS - for their generous provision of ribbon,
fabrics and threads.

FABRIC FLAIR - for providing fabric for the
evening bag and waistcoat.

ROGER FALCON - for framing the pictures.

FRAMECRAFT - for the silver dressing table set.

IMPRESS CARDS - for card samples.

ANN PEPPRELL of 'Threads & So Much More'
- for silk and satin ribbons.

RIBBON DESIGNS - for silk ribbons.

PAT ROWLAND - for making up the garden etui.

SELECTUS - for their generous contribution of Panda ribbons.

'Poppies and Daisies' (page 112) was originally featured in the July/August 1994 edition
of *Classic Stitches* magazine published by D.C. Thomson & Co. Ltd.

'Oval Mauves' (page 48) was originally featured in the September 1994 edition of
Needlework magazine published by Aspen Litharne Publishing.

Index